Mohanji
FOUNDATION

Guru Leela
Volume 3
Grace that Heals

This book is a **Mohanji Satcharita** -
a collection of honest testimonials from
devotees across the globe

Compiled & Edited By
Mohanji Testimonials Team

https://mohanjichronicles.wordpress.com/
testimonials@mohanji.org

Copyright 2020 Mohanji Foundation
(www.mohanji.org, Facebook page: MohanjiOfficial)
All Rights Reserved

No part of this book may be reproduced,
or stored in a retrieval system,
or transmitted by
any means without the
written permission of the author.

**Guru Leela - Volume 3
Grace that Heals**

ISBN No.: 978-81-935309-5-5
MRP: Rs. 400 (in India only)

First Edition:
Published by GuruLight, 2020
www.gurulight.com

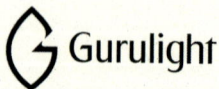

Acknowledgments & Credits
Cover Design: Mohana Hanumantananda
Content layout: Span Communications
Printed by: Usha Multigraphs Pvt. Ltd., Mumbai
Transcription, Editing & Proof Reading:
Rekha Murali, Shyama Jeyaseelan
Publication Coordination: Subhasree Thottungal

Grace that Heals

A friend whom you can trust

We dedicate this book, **'Guru Leela - Grace that Heals'** to Mohanji with immense gratitude and love. May these true and life-transforming testimonials of healing with divine grace, bring peace and happiness to all those who read this book.

Mohanji
FOUNDATION

*with Love
Mohanji*

CONTENTS

From The Editors' Pen i

Forewords

With Love From Greenland vi
Angaangaq Angakkorsuaq

Super Hero xi
Ana Divac

I Treat, He Heals xvi
Dr Harpreet Wasir

When The Master's Grace Heals 1
Devi Mohan, Slovenia

Incurable To Being Cured 19
Arpana Nazre, India

Divine Call Of Nature 30
Cathy Johnston, UK

A Friend For Life 43
A devotee, India

An Extended Lease 47
A devotee, UK

Healing Touch 54
Elham Khordadian, USA

On Healing And Letting Go 56
Hein Adamson, India

Glimpses Of Miracles 60
Ivana Kodzic, Serbia

Mohanji And My Mother 70
Jyoti Bahl, India

Saving Grace 77
Lai Siong Chai, UK

Magical Healing In Machu Picchu 81
Livia, Netherlands

Birth Of True Self 90
Milica Bulatovic, South Africa

A Date With Destiny 100
Natesh Ramsell, USA

A Gift Of A New Life! 108
Neelima Vepu, India

Inner Truth 112
NellyAnne Noronha, UK

From Self-hate To Self-Acceptance 118
Nikolina Dragojević, Serbia

Miracles Of Grace 125
Nirupma Chowdhary, India

The Magnificent Surgeon 134
Preeti Duggal, India

From Darkness To Light 138
Rakshitha Ananth, Australia

Anchored In Love	146
Rekha Murali, India	
A Precious Gift	152
Saakshi Gupta, India	
Invisible Embrace	157
Subhasree Thottungal, UK	
A Walk Of Faith	168
Sunita Madan, India	
The Unseen Healer	171
Tina Arya, USA	
Cosmic Wink	174
Charice Bhardwaj, UK	
Woh Saans	179
Devotional Song – Jyoti Bahl	

Disclaimer:

"The views, opinions and positions expressed by the authors on these testimonials are theirs alone, and do not necessarily reflect the views, opinions or positions of Mohanji, Mohanji Foundation, its members, employees or any other individual or entity associated with Mohanji or Mohanji Foundation. We make no representations as to accuracy, completeness, timeliness, suitability or validity of any information presented by individual authors and will not be liable for any errors, omissions, or delays in this information or any losses, injuries or damages arising from its display or use."

Mohanji Testimonials Team

FROM THE EDITORS' PEN

With the blessings and grace of our beloved Mohanji, we are very happy to be publishing the third book in the Guru Leela series, Guru Leela Volume 3 – Grace that Heals. Every experience shared in this book is a loving offering from the hearts of those who have been healed in various ways, physically, mentally, emotionally or spiritually by Mohanji's powerful and divine energy. Some of these extraordinary events and miraculous experiences will leave the readers filled with awe. Our deepest gratitude to Mohanji for his eternal love and protection; present not only for his devotees but also for their families and lineage.

Grace that heals is a collection of stories where people from different walks of life have experienced healing through various aspects of Mohanji. Healing can happen in his physical presence/energy field or by connecting to him through prayer, chanting or remembrance. Other ways of connecting with Mohanji's energy are through the Mai-Tri Method and Mohanji Transformation Method. These are profound methods of deep cleansing, balancing, harmonising and rejuvenation which greatly enhance the natural self-healing abilities of the recipient. Through these methods, the initiated practitioners connect with the consciousness of Mohanji.

Hundreds of devotees from all over the world seek the presence and blessings of Mohanji. When we connect to him with honesty and sincerity, he takes care of every one, directly or indirectly, taking away our troubles and sufferings. Guiding us on our individual journeys, and bringing about positive inner transformations, Mohanji works tirelessly to help all beings of the world. He is the most compassionate companion and the truest friend who would never let go of our hands.

Mohanji was recently described as follows in a European publication:

> *"Mohanji is not a mystic.*
> *He is a friend whom you can trust."*

This trust is what we feel the most when in his physical presence. His gentle smile, kind eyes and the warm hug wrap us in an aura of love and protection, enabling us to share our deepest troubles with him. With a casual hug, he heals us on all levels and removes blockages of lifetimes. In an unassuming way, this trusted friend works on every aspect of our being, cleansing us, giving us what we need, and walks with us on our chosen path. This grace of healing happens when we connect with Mohanji sincerely from the heart, and he takes care of the rest. As he often says,

> *"Keep walking.*
> *I am walking with you."*

Devi Amma, a living Saint of the Tradition, very clearly shared,

> "He is Vishwa Mitra –
> A friend of the Universe."

Under this physical connection as a friend is a Master whom we can only catch a glimpse of, through the various experiences and transformations that happen within us. This too is visible only if we have the eyes to see and have the awareness from within. He works effortlessly and quietly, unseen and unheard. He is a daya sagar – an ocean of mercy and compassion. His love has no boundaries of space and time. Everyone benefits and anyone can take shelter under his umbrella of grace and protection.

Our heartfelt gratitude to all those who have contributed towards creating this book, it is a beautiful offering of love to our eternal guide, protector and friend, Mohanji. This gratitude is the reason behind the birth of this Guru Leela series. It is a humble attempt to present a collection of beautiful experiences of devotees from around the world, through which we get a glimpse of this beautiful incarnation known as Mohanji. May this set of true stories be handed over to future generations also, to know about this divine being who walked this Earth.

As Mohanji says, writing and sharing our transformative experiences is very important.

> "When you experience grace in life, write your memoirs. When you are in despair and cannot feel the grace factor, you can read that. Your own experiences are your greatest assets. Your own life is your most reliable guide." Mohanji

We hope all the readers feel the power of Mohanji's divine leela and his grace while reading these stories. After reading this book, please send your feedback to **'testimonials@mohanji.org.'**

Our heartfelt gratitude to the authors and contributors of each article in this book. They have transformed this book into a beautiful expression of grace that heals.

We extend our sincere gratitude to Angaangaq Angakkorsuaq, Inuit Kalaallit, Great Shaman – Greenland, for writing a letter with love to Mohanji.

Our heartfelt thanks to Ana Divac for her honest sharing about Mohanji in the **'Foreword – Super Hero'**.

We are grateful to Dr Harpreet Wasir for his inspiring and honest sharing in his **'Foreword – I treat, he heals'**.

Our deepest appreciation to the book presentation team: Mohana Hanumatananda for the cover page design, Venkatraman K. V. for the book layout design and Sarathy Raghavan for the printing and consultation.

Above all, Thank you to Mohanji for being our invisible guide throughout this journey, without whom, this would not have been a reality.

With love,

Rekha Murali, Shyama Jeyaseelan and
Subhasree Thottungal

|| **Jai Brahmarishi Mohanji** ||

WITH LOVE FROM GREENLAND
Angaangaq Angakkorsuaq

Angaangaq Angakkorsuaq is a Shaman, traditional healer, Storyteller and a carrier of the Qilaut (wind drum). His family belongs to the traditional healers from Kalaallit Nunaat, Greenland. His engagement for the environment and indigenous issues brought him to more than 70 countries in the world.

Mohanji and Angaangaq Angakkorsuaq share a beautiful and loving friendship based on their love for Mother Earth and all her beings. Having worked together during the Peace Pledge in 2018 and 2019, their friendship continues to grow with a common focus – to help the world. The letter below is a loving message from Angaangaq Angakkorsuaq to Mohanji, his close friend.

My dear friend and younger brother Mohanji,

I know that people are writing a book of experiences about you and I wanted to contribute something to that as you and I have travelled together and met each other over the years. You where young when I first met you, I don't know if you remember that. But we travelled to my land in Greenland, and then you saw what is happening to the world in which we live. The spiritual significance of climate change is something nobody really wants to talk about. Mostly because they don't believe in it or most likely they don't understand the significance of it.

Your land, this amazing country called India is such an important place on earth. Why? Because there are so many people who live there. Your land would also be one of the first countries in the world which will have a severe impact due to climate change, most importantly with regards to water. In my language, water is called 'Imeq' which literally means: 'life-giving source of all.' Now we have learned through science that water is a life-giving source of all, not just because our body contains a lot of water.

But then we live in a world where we don't understand what is happening to our earth and the impact we have on this earth. We have talked about it, and you saw for yourself what was happening in Greenland.

The spiritual significance of climate change is something which is so essential for the well-being of all of us on earth; which means the humans, animals, plants and minerals. None of these four components can live without water. And all of them need clean water, and we have failed in that. The spiritual leaders of the world of which you are a part of, are really important for the well-being of mankind.

We have now gone beyond religion, it's no longer a religious issue and in fact, it has never been a religious issue. But it's always been a spiritual issue. Because no matter what we believe in, and there are many kinds of beliefs, in the spirit, it's always the same, where ever I go. I may not have travelled as much as you have, but I have worked in 72 different countries on this earth. And I have visited thousands of cities in the world to talk about the melting of the Big Ice, and the severity of the impact she will carry which will affect the spiritual well-being of mankind.

My prayer is that in your work, being young and vibrant, you will focus on that spiritual significance. Because, without that, we will get lost. What does it mean to get lost? We will begin to talk about religion rather than spiritual well-being and as you know, when we talk about religion, we always end up arguing. But when we talk about the spiritual significance, beautiful smiles are born from every heart. Because then we can look at each other as equals. That's the work you do, and that's the one thing which is most important.

Whatever book is being published about you, the way I see you is that you bring the spirit alive in every person. I look forward to the day when we can sit down again and have our coffee together. And this time go further deep within us to understand that there's no difference amongst us, no matter where we come from, no matter what conditions we come from, and no matter what aspirations we have. All we want is people to understand the beauty and the significance of water on earth. Love you so much.

Angaangaq Angakkorsuaq
Inuit Kalaallit Great Shaman from
the top of the world - Greenland.

Grace that Heals

*Those who are grateful are also graceful.
They are filled with grace.*

Guru Leela

A randezvous with Mohanji.

SUPER HERO

Ana Divac

Ana Divac is the founder member of 'Ana & Vlade Foundation', the number one philanthropist foundation of Serbia. Wife of the former National Basketball champion Vlade Divac, Ana is also a popular media celebrity and actress. Her contribution to society through many projects that she and her husband support is inspiring to many. Since she met Mohanji, she has experienced personal transformations that have helped even more in her service towards society. Ana has gladly expressed her feelings for Mohanji in this write-up below.

"A Superhero is a person who does heroic deeds and has the ability to do them in a way that a normal person couldn't. So in order to be a superhero, you need a power that is more exceptional than any power a normal human being could possess, and you need to use that power to accomplish good deeds. Otherwise, a policeman or a fireman could be considered a superhero. For instance, a good guy fighting a bad guy could be just a regular police story or detective story or human-interest story. But if it's a good guy with a superpower who is fighting a bad guy, it becomes a superhero story. If the good guy is doing something that a normal human being couldn't do, couldn't accomplish, then I assume he becomes a superhero." - Stan Lee

So, we already have all these superheroes. In Eastern culture, they are mostly worshiped, and in Western culture we are more practical, we are in contact with them through comic books, games, and films.

But one thing is common. In the East and the West, the North and the South, we need superheroes to make sense of the reality we live in, which unfortunately is mostly non-understanding, separation from each other and ourselves, injustice, cruelty, and war.

These superheroes give us hope that we can reach a state of unity, understanding, acceptance of others and ourselves, the ability to discover the power inside of us, and to love.

For me, Mohanji has all the characteristics of a superhero. He has superpowers, but is as human as I am. I try to understand how he does it all. How does he manage to be with hundreds of people at the same time without being physically present? And how does he hear me when I need help? There were times I thought I understood, and then the next day nothing would make sense again. I gave up trying to understand, and doing so became less important to me. I just know that I could feel him. That he's always there for me. Both, when I love him the most and when I am angry with him for not working the way I want him to, for not fulfilling my desires in the form and timeline that I envisioned, when I doubt if all this makes sense, and when I wonder, what is the point?

I always know he's there for me. Much more than I am there for myself, when I don't think I can do it anymore, when I'm scared and when it gets too hard. Although I have to admit that I also feel his presence when I'm having a great time, and when I'm well with myself and everyone that I don't need anything.

I have helped many people in my life. I can even say that when I've been in a position to answer the requests, I've helped everyone who has ever asked me for help. Many times I have been hurt by the people I helped. I didn't want their gratitude, I wanted them to be good and that brought me joy. But I couldn't understand how they could undo and forget my loving care and effort. This is the trait I have most condemned in people. Since this life rings us insights about ourselves, that we are all that which we least love and condemn in others, thanks to Mohanji, I have seen it in myself.

It's easier for me when I tell myself 'well, that's just your mind.' But I think it would be okay for me to finally come to an agreement with my mind to stop doing this to me and show me the true data, which is what Mohanji did for me. For example, I would think of just one fact, after 15 years of torturing and wandering from doctors to various types of healers, I would be healed thanks to him. Or that maybe my daughter was left with just four scars on her leg instead of losing her leg altogether after a car accident. Or for the first time, none of the five of us, since we've existed as a family, had a fight during the Christmas holidays. Anyone who is close to us knows that this is a pure miracle and that there is definitely an influence of some superpowers.

And the list of what Mohanji has done for me, my family and my friends is ever growing. I keep telling myself that I will start writing because the moment we are transformed and the transformation becomes a part of our reality; we forget that we were ever different. And of course, we focus on what we still don't have.

Guru Leela

Somehow I think my life would get uncomfortably small if I didn't have Mohanji in it. I know he says that he is in me and in all of us and I understand the meaning of it, but I'm glad to be able to see him, smell him, and hug him. I'm glad to also have the physical proof that a superhero really exists.

His superpower is an unconditional love that transforms everyone around him or connected to him. And to be honest, until I felt that power of unconditional love, I might have chosen Superman or Punisher or Batman first. But now I know that unconditional love is the greatest superpower and that through it, all miracles happen.

Mohanji does not give up on us, even when we are at our worst, when we make the same mistakes over and over again, and when we do not trust ourselves. He leads us to start seeing ourselves and others through his eyes, the eyes of love.

For there to be drama and for the superhero to forego losing his job, villains must exist as well. And they have superpowers too. Most are found within our minds. Usually they are in the form of expectations, unacceptance, condemnation, and ungratefulness. One of their greatest superpower is doubt that a superheroes exist, and that we with our regular human traits don't have a chance against them. And through that doubt they separate us. But whoever has had the chance to feel Mohanji's superpower, unconditional love, and whoever has ever seen a superhero film can know for a fact that in the end, after all the drama and fights, the superhero always wins.

Please watch the video interview with Mohanji by Ana through this link.

https://mohanji.org/ana-divac-show/

I TREAT, HE HEALS

Dr Harpreet Wasir

Dr Wasir is a cardiac surgeon in one of the prestigious hospitals in New Delhi, India. After connecting to Mohanji for more than five years, he expresses his transformation that has brought a positive impact on his treatment of patients. Inspired by Mohanji's teachings of compassion, kindness and selfless service, Dr Wasir has been involved in many selfless activities with Ammucare, Healers Beyond Boundaries and the latest project in Arunachala - Mohanji Home for Seniors, by providing them with regular medical services.

I am so honoured to have an opportunity to write a foreword for this book "Guru Leela – Volume 3, Grace that Heals." Blessed is this book which shares all aspects of healing through Guru's grace.

Even though I am a doctor by profession, I truly believe that irrespective of the profession, everyone is a healer in a true sense. However, when a Guru walks into our lives, a turning point happens as we then receive a GPS - Guru Protection System. Through Guru's leelas, an understanding of the Guru's grace comes in.

With Guru's grace, we lose our blockages and trapped impressions. What increases are our awareness and acceptance. This is what I understood when my Guru Mohanji walked into my life. I learnt that Mohanji has come into my life not to tell me how to grow, but to teach me what more I can give back to society. This is the only way we can reduce our karmic baggage and cut short on our rebirths and sufferings. Mohanji taught me to experience liberation while living and ultimately that will bring liberation while leaving. This is Guru's leela if you ask me. Simple basic fact.

I came with nothing and I wish to leave with nothing. No ownership. This thought process/awareness has been a turning point for me even in my profession as a doctor. I give my Guru to my patients with a big open heart. When I hold their hand, I feel that Mohanji is holding their hand. When I put my hand on their head, I feel Mohanji is giving them the feeling of a higher power.

I treat, he heals.

When Mohanji is taking care of them, what then comes is a spontaneous flow of compassion and kindness. When I surrender my patients to Mohanji, I know he is taking care. I am not the doer and hence the results are not mine. With a continuous connection to Mohanji's consciousness, what then comes is an enormous amount of energy. There is no compromise on hard work.

It is miraculously beyond what a logical mind can describe or medical science can explain, through connection to Mohanji's consciousness, patients not only get treated, but they also get healed. Patients come at the right time, correct decisions are made, and the correct treatments are offered. Still no ownership, just acceptance. In the field of cardiac surgery, where one is playing with life and death, to keep calm and to follow the path of acceptance and surrender is not that easy, but it becomes possible only through Guru's grace.

The key message is acceptance, then surrender and finally, it's walking the Guru's path as the rest slowly dissolves.

This book, Guru Leela, is not about the authors. Each sharing is a lesson in itself. Every time a chapter is read, a new awareness comes in and the distance towards liberation is shortened. Mohanji speaks and teaches us through all these experiences. He makes it so simple for us. As he says, "All that you have to do is to plug in, the rest is my job." These stories are all about 'plugging in' and the rest is taken care of by him to the fullest.

The reading of this book is evidence of Guru's grace and brings healing to the reader. This book carries the divine energy of Mohanji, as do all the previous books in the Guru Leela series.

All from him, and all to him.

Grace that Heals

If you love yourself, you will never leave me because I am yourself, your own beautiful, eternal, unforgettable creation.

Guru Leela

WHEN THE MASTER'S GRACE HEALS

Devi Mohan, Slovenia

As I sit down to write my thoughts, a thousand faces travel through my mind - the faces of all those whom Mohanji has touched over the last thirteen years since I have known him (in this lifetime). He has inspired, empowered and transformed thousands of people across the globe, blessing them with exactly what they were lacking to evolve further. Some recognized the depth of the blessing they have received, and some took it as a mere coincidence that their life transformed in some positive way or that certain healing had happened after meeting Mohanji. Since he is so unassuming, the most natural thing is to take him for granted. It takes a lot of maturity to recognize the depth of a Master and how he operates.

When it comes to healing, it is only one small expression of a profound transformative work that a Master of Mohanji's stature does for any deserving disciple. Mohanji often says: "Healing is my visiting card." Indeed, what a true spiritual Master does for a disciple can't be compared to any physical healing. The transformation leading to spiritual liberation beyond this lifetime is the true task of Masters. This is so incomparably greater than any physical healing. And yet, it is the healing that first catches the attention of a disciple and opens the door to surrender, devotion and faith. That is why healing is often used as the visiting card.

When Mohanji first came to my parental home in Novi Sad, Serbia, in 2008, he shared his visiting card with my parents and relatives in the most unassuming, utterly sweet way. Unlike the usual future sons-in-law, Mohanji was not making any effort whatsoever to leave a positive impression on his future in-laws. When no question came his way, he would quietly sit on the sofa, smiling from within. My father was not happy to hear that there was no point in offering his meat delicacies or his favorite plum brandy to my fiancé. I told him that Mohanji is vegan and that he doesn't drink alcohol. However, regardless of those glaring shortcomings, my father quickly got to like him because he had no airs about his eating habits. On the contrary, he was very natural and easily approachable.

At one point, my father sat next to him and started talking about the usual subject of the elderly – long stories about his past and complaints about his health. What troubled my father the most at that time was his right shoulder. It hurt so much that he couldn't even move his hand properly, not to mention lifting it up. My father showed Mohanji how he couldn't lift his elbow, not even to shoulder height. There was some strange pain in his shoulder which puzzled the doctors because nothing concrete was visible on the usual body scans. Mohanji asked my father if he could hold his right wrist. He then placed his fingertips on the inner part of the wrist and started transmitting energy for a minute or so. I was wondering where he had learned this ayurvedic pulse diagnostics from, all of a sudden. However, later on, I understood that Mohanji was anyway looking through the third eye to see the root cause of this shoulder issue and would be passing on the healing energy with or without any touch. But by placing his fingertips on my Dad's wrist, he made it look more acceptable. He whispered to me that it's all about the past-life impression of being stabbed in his shoulder, but I should not tell him that. At some point, Mohanji removed his fingers and my father started moving his arm to see if there was any difference. Suddenly he shouted: "Look! See this! I can move my arm. This is unbelievable! Look how far I can lift it!" He kept showing how far his hand could go and his joy had no end. Excitement filled the room.

We were supposed to leave for the airport soon and I got busy with packing. My aunt from Croatia approached Mohanji and asked whether he could help her as well. She had multiple fractures in her right arm due to a car accident more than a year ago, but the pain was still there. Mohanji asked to hold her wrist as well. Everybody looked attentively. When he removed his hand, my aunt had a big smile on her face and said: "I can't feel any pain. It is gone. Wow, thank you so much."

Karmic law of healing

I noticed one thing about Mohanji that I admire a lot – even when he was in great pain and distress, or in great financial crisis, he would not ask Masters to help him. He asked nothing for himself and never used his third eye for his own benefit. I once asked him why can't he during any of his communions with the Masters, seek their help in some tough situations. He answered: **"I know that Masters are**

with me all the time and I surrender to their willfully. If I am to go through some experiences for the purpose of karmic cleansing, so be it. Otherwise, what surrender are we talking about?"

While living with Mohanji, I started observing more closely how the karmic laws work. I came to understand that healing can happen only if that specific pain or health issue is not a part of one's prarabdha karma (the destiny aspect of karma, meaning that what we as souls chose to go through in this life, for whatever reason). **"You can have pain, but you need not have suffering. That part is a choice"**, was Mohanji's usual comment about pain. He once had kidney stones and had to go for an intervention of breaking them with the help of a laser. This is a very painful process which usually requires anaesthesia, but not in Mohanji's case. He was telling me once about this in his lighthearted, humorous way: "I told them to tell me when they will start and how long the whole procedure will last. The moment they stared, I left my body, very simple. I re-entered the body after the time they said they needed was over, but the procedure was still going on. Phew, there was pain! Wrong timing, so I went out of the body again for some more time." It was all a play for him.

One time, Mohanji, my sister Dana, and I drove from Dubai to a tourist location an hour or so away. It was a nice day and all went beautifully but at some point, I suddenly started having a strong intuition that we were about to have a car accident. The road was curvy and I started feeling the chills in my body. I felt that it would happen any minute and became dead silent. Interestingly enough, my sister shared with me later on that she had felt it as well. It felt like time was skewed and one could not distinguish whether the accident happened, is happening, or will happen, but the feeling was there big time. Mohanji was on the co-driver's seat, completely silent, holding the handle above the window tightly. The two of us were in the back, getting very restless. And then suddenly the uncomfortable feeling vanished. I felt light and very relieved. It was then that I noticed something interesting – there was an inch-long cut on Mohanji's hand which appeared out of nowhere. It was not bleeding but it was a visible cut. There was nothing around Mohanji's hand that could cause this cut. I was perplexed but understood right away that this cut represented our car accident. He took that karma onto himself and instead of us going through the drama and pain of the car accident; he had reduced it into this cut. That was only the beginning of me witnessing many situations in which Mohanji hugged someone or tapped someone and took some pain of that person onto himself. He would still have to go through some of it, but it was much reduced. Such is the grace of the Divine that works through the Masters.

In the initial days, when I started living with Mohanji, he continued to be a mystery to me. He was having profound insights, communions and various experiences beyond the comprehension of the human mind. The more I knew him, the more I realized that I do not know him... He enjoyed acting like a common person, like someone ignorant of even the basics of spirituality. At some other times, however, he would surprise everyone by delivering intense, transformative experiences, sharing profound insights or by making the impossible happen. Slowly, but steadily, I started understanding the man behind this illusion.

Mohanji belongs to the profound tradition of Dattatreya. All the saints of this Tradition are unique. None like another. Lord Dattatreya himself is unique. He is the unity in trinity. He is the incarnation of Parabrahma, the Almighty. Mohanji often recommends people to chant **"Aum Parabrahmane Namaha"** – "To know the unity, see Parabrahma in everything. He is the non-dual Truth." As I started understanding the Tradition that Mohanji represents, I realised how difficult this path is. It is simple and tough; simple - because there are no rigid rules and practices; tough - because the duality always obscures the vision of unity. And Masters are all too unassuming and invisible. To realize or understand a Datta Guru is very difficult. Only the one who has his/her third eye active can comprehend his glory. Datta Gurus always confused people with their mannerisms and thus elevated them by their sheer presence. Tons of karma gets washed away by just being around a Datta Master. Moreover, they live a life of perfection, while being completely natural and transparent. Shirdi Sai Baba is a great example. And yet at times, they behave in a bizarre manner which confuses people to believe that they are mad. Diversity is the expression of life, finding unity within that diversity is the mission and goal of human existence. I realized this through Mohanji.

Mila's fall

When our daughter Mila fell from a height of 4 - 5 meters onto a marble floor in Nov 2013, I experienced pain incomparable to anything else I've ever experienced. I have been through a war, the humiliations of being a refugee, risked my life daily while working for the UN in Kosovo and went through a near-death experience, but nothing could be compared to this. Any parent would gladly trade his/her life for that of a child. The way Mohanji handled this situation is something I will never forget – after three days in ICU, we were able to 'bounce back' and even went onto the stage during the ACT Fusion concert, dressed up in colorful clothes, as if nothing had happened. This experience was truly magical.

Witnessing Mila's fall was the most painful and horrible experience of my life. I went to a 5-star hotel in Delhi with a couple of our friends and Mila intending to discuss the fundraising possibilities with the hotel's Human Resources Manager. While waiting for the meeting, like any 3-year-old, Mila was curious and enjoyed exploring this new environment. When she ran outside, I noticed that she entered the grass area surrounding the main yard of the hotel. It had a gradual slope covered by grass, with a green bush fence at the top. I was happy that she was not going anywhere near the fountain, so I allowed her to run on the grass. It looked safe. However, Mila started climbing up towards the top where the bush fence was. I kept shouting: "Mila, come back! You can't go there. Come back!" but she kept giggling and ran up the small hill. I gave up on the idea of sparing my fancy shoes with high heels from entering the grass and started running after her. She reached the top, looked at me with a smile, and then as if something pulled her hair from the back, she simply disappeared. As I was climbing up, I noticed that the fence was not continuous as it seemed from the yard. There was an opening between the green bushes and a stone arch next to it. I looked through the area between the bush fence and the stone arch and witnessed a scene I will never forget – my beloved baby spread out on a marble floor way, way down (more than 4 meters of height).

She was lying on her back on that marble floor and did not seem to be alive. I couldn't digest this situation. For a moment, I felt that I was no longer in my body but suddenly out of my body, hovering above Mila. For a couple of seconds, I was in a detached witnessing state (that I recognize from my near-death experience in 2000) ready to cross over with her. It felt as if less than 20% of me was still connected with the body. At some point, that part of me pushed back. A thought came: "Maybe she is still alive, maybe there is a chance to go back to the life we had." I decide to make an effort to call for help urgently, to see whether Mila can still be saved. That small part of me willed the bigger floating part back into the physical body. However, no sound would come from my mouth. I tried to shout for help, but no voice came. Then I squatted a bit and with the full force of my hip flexor muscles suddenly straightened my body and managed to produce a loud yell "Help!" Oblivious to the fact that there was a stone arch above my head while straightening my legs in that super strong way, I hit my head exactly at the sensitive area of the crown chakra. I was so preoccupied with Mila's situation that I did not feel much pain, just suddenly felt warm blood gushing down my head. I bent forward and continued shouting while the blood was falling from my head through a 3 cm long cut straight onto the grass. The pain and fear that I felt for Mila were so great that it overshadowed any physical pain that I could have had. I couldn't care less about my body.

Hotel guards responded immediately – one ran around the building to get Mila and one brought a small towel for me to press it against my head. In less than twenty seconds, I held my beloved Mila in my arms relieved to see that she was conscious, but in a lot of pain. She kept making a moaning sound. Very soon a car arrived, ready to take us to a nearby hospital right away.

The minutes of reaching the hospital seemed like an eternity in hell – I fought the mind's pull towards negative thoughts like, "Will she ever walk again? Will she remain sane?" trying to focus on my breath. But the mind kept bombarding me: "Your stupid high heels. You should have run after her. It's all your fault. Now she is finished. She will never be the same again." I fought these horrible thoughts but nothing worked until I started chanting fervently: "Om Sai, Shri Sai, Jai Jai Sai!" I kept repeating this, overpowering the destructive, evil thoughts that I was bombarded with. I felt immense fear that I may be holding Mila in the wrong way, so worried about the spine and possible life-long consequences of not keeping her body straight at this critical time. She wanted me to hold her tight, but with one hand I had to hold the towel on top of my head because I was still bleeding a lot. After reaching the hospital, further traumas ensued – as I placed Mila on the bed in the Emergency Room, a big strand of her hair suddenly remained in my palm. It scared me and I did not know what to make out of it. However, intuitively I knew that this strand of hair was plucked by whoever/whichever entity that pulled Mila's hair and caused her to fall backwards onto the ground. A couple of moments later, the doctor asked me to hold her up to see whether she can walk. My heart broke when I saw the wobbly legs. However, 2 – 3 seconds later Mila suddenly starting kicking with both her legs, annoyed by the uncomfortable position. That brought a deep, deep sigh of relief.

The doctor said that her body seemed to be OK but there was a visible bump (hematoma) on the back of her head, the part that endured the strongest hit during the fall. This bump meant that internal bleeding was surely happening, which is very dangerous because accumulated blood had already started pressing the brain and that is very dangerous. The doctor said that considering the height from which she fell, brain surgery may be required urgently. However, that can be determined only after the brain scan.

Mohanji arrived, along with his sweet parents who were pale and silent. Having survived the trauma of losing Ammu thirteen years ago, I could not even imagine how painful it would have been for them to re-open those wounds and face such pain again.

Grace that Heals

This is when the prayers started. All of us were in continuous, fervent prayer for Mila, knowing that the outcome of the brain scan was in the hands of the Divine. In the next 3 hours, the second brain scan would decide the further course of action.

I remember the moment when Mohanji sat next to Mila's bed and placed his hand on her head. My eyes fixated on his facial expression. There were no emotions visible on his face, only the depth of focus within. At that moment somebody took a photo of him and Mila and posted it on Facebook, which is not something we would have ever wanted. However, the good thing was that the word about Mila's fall spread very fast among all our friends and family and so many were sending loving rays of light and healing to Mila through their deep prayers.

At last, the result of the second brain scan came – even though there were two hematomas, the internal bleeding had started to subside rapidly and it was established that the brain surgery won't be required. The doctor said that this was nothing short of a miracle! I looked at Mohanji and saw his stern and serious face. He, later on, confirmed to me what I had felt deep inside – he took the karma of death due to brain haemorrhage (at whichever point in physical time), onto himself. He shared with me later on that, when he placed his hands on her head, the energy pull through the hand was so strong that for some time, his hand felt literally glued to her head. The required energy transmission happened. Mila was saved.

I must say that it was appalling to me that some

people came to the hospital mainly to see how Mohanji would react. They came to test him. Such is human nature.

After all this was over, both Mila and I were kept in the ICU under strict observation for three days. Mila was given IV fluids and she could not stand those needles. Used to homeopathy, all this was completely new to her and very unpleasant. We could not sleep at all due to an old man next to us, who was gasping for air loudly and literally dying right there. Only the next day did we get a separate room for another two days and finally enjoyed some sleep. We happily left the hospital a day before the ACT Fusion charity concert, which was the main reason for our trip to Delhi.

On the day of the ACT Fusion concert, holding Mila in my arms, I climbed on the stage and spoke, feeling indescribably grateful that I got my life back, my dreams back, that the nightmare was over and a beautiful life filled with grace, service and love continues.

Observed from a grand perspective, I am aware that all our experiences have a higher meaning and if this experience was meant to strengthen my faith and gratitude and gain further clarity about the challenges and beauty on this amazing spiritual path of ours, so be it.

I am forever grateful to all our friends who contributed to Mila's speedy recovery with their prayers, blessings and loving wishes, which certainly did reach her. In the lap of our Grand Tradition, in the lap of the Divine, and through utmost love and selflessness of her beloved father Mohanji, Mila's healing took place miraculously. I have no words to describe the depth, beauty, love and selflessness that Mohanji demonstrated through this act of purest love. All I can say is that we are forever grateful for the blessing of Mohanji's physical presence in our lives.

The mighty radiance of our Tradition shines forth

It took us some time to digest this entire experience fully. During the conversations that I had with Mohanji after the accident, he shared with me some profound insights about our path. He taught me the following lessons, which I will always remember and treasure:

"No entity can affect me directly. But beware; they could affect me through you or Mila, or others who are close to me or my mission. If you are within my energy field and consciousness, you are safe. Otherwise, you are vulnerable. Their aim is to slow me down. This has happened to almost all the Masters of the past. Many roadblocks have been created in their path systematically so that they would slow down. Even negative thoughts are given to their followers so that they are distracted and leave the path. The other path option is a path of comfort zones, fears and bindings."

"There are numerous teachers and very few Masters on Earth today. The Masters are connected to the Source. They are the target. The teachers are not affected. Jesus was connected to the Source. He was killed. Socrates and Osho were connected to the Source. Those who are connected to the Source are taking people from earthly bindings to the path of liberation. Most of them are Avadhootas. Shirdi Sai was even taken to court when he was in his body. Hence, being my wife, you have a very high responsibility. You should be connected to my consciousness always and operate in that. This is very important to know because, if they want to slow me down, they may use you for that. It is your responsibility to always remain connected and then you are safe." He then continued about Mila:

"Mila is Mohanji's daughter and it is not easy for her. Lord Krishna, Jesus and all the higher souls had a tough childhood. How many beings attacked Krishna when he was a baby? The parents of Jesus had to go abroad to save the life of their child. The more powerful the entity, the more vulnerable is the person affected. Ammu was powerful as well. We know that now, as she is continuously working through many people to wipe the tears of many through Ammucare/ACT. They will certainly leave their impression on Earth irrespective of their time on this planet. But, it is the extraordinary responsibility of the parents to take care of the baby. You cannot take chances."

"The Nath Tradition or the Datta Tradition is powerful. Once someone is connected to it, he/she will always be protected. But, this path is the path of liberation and hence, everyone's free will is well respected. The door of the Tradition always stays swinging open for people to come, stay and if they choose, to go. Once inside the house, they are well taken care of."

Baba's special gift for Mila

From all my past experiences with the Great Sai, I know that whenever he performs a miracle, he also makes sure a concrete 'evidence' or sign is given to confirm the same to our doubting mind.

Well, no more proofs are required in this body-mind-soul system my dearest Baba – I am yours and you live in my heart forever.

After leaving Delhi, Mohanji happened to meet Vittal Babaji, a powerful living Master from the Datta Tradition. I was deeply touched when Mohanji shared with me the loving words of Vittal Babaji:

"Mila is the child of our Tradition, the powerful Datta Tradition. She is the child of all the Masters of this Tradition. Nobody can harm her permanently. Out of jealousy, they will try. But, she is well within our protection ring. Being Mohanji's child, she would be too visible to the world. She will always be protected by the Masters."

Many people claim they can connect with God, that is, the Formless Absolute, through their prayers, as per the directions/conditionings of their faith. However, I do believe that unless the Divine consciousness comes with a form and one first connects to that form through deep experiences and iron-strong faith, he/she cannot develop faith in the Formless unless truly blessed through direct experience. In critical times especially, during the harshest of tests, this generalized faith towards the Formless Absolute fails us. The Divine in human form serves the purpose in preparing us to comprehend the Formless Absolute, the Father, Allah, or Parabramha, whichever name one wants to use.

If we are to experience deep fulfillment in our life at all levels, there is only one requirement – a deep desire to be an instrument of this purest possible love, to live it, to express it, to serve it – and eventually, to become one with it.

May all of us be blessed with the courage and determination required to tread the pathless path, the path of liberation, with utmost faith and surrender.

Grace that Heals

Guru Leela

INCURABLE TO BEING CURED

Arpana Nazre, India

I have been in the IT industry for quite a long time now. Along with it come the stress, project deadlines, late nights, long hours, working weekends, sedentary lifestyle, competition, and politics. Everything you can think of, that could affect your body in some way or the other. The longer you are here, the more damage it causes. If a balance is not made, it can even be fatal to your physical and mental health. Of course there are good things too, like money, stability, etc. However, here I would like to write how the industry and other factors triggered an ailment on my physical being.

A couple of years back, I was in a very good project, but at the same time, very demanding and taxing. Extremely stressful, working late nights, and a very demanding superior, added to the woes. Also, it was a Canadian project, so most of the meetings used to happen late in the nights. This went on for almost a year and a half. By the end of the year, I started developing painful joints. Thinking that it was due to sitting for long hours in front of the computer, I just neglected it. Whenever I used to get up from my seat after sitting for long, my joints would be stiff, and I would almost limp to even go to the nearest bathroom. Over time, it started getting worse. My knees would become swollen. I couldn't get down from the vehicle and walk after driving to office. Slowly, my ankle joints, elbows, shoulder joints, everything started showing signs of inflammation and pain. A time came when I finally had to visit the doctor. After the initial tests, the doctor suspected Rheumatoid Arthritis (referred to RA henceforth).

I was hoping that it would be something minor and would be healed with a little medication. But as fate would have it, the blood reports confirmed Rheumatoid Arthritis. Until then, I knew nothing about it. Upon further investigation (thanks to google), to my horror, I realised that it's a chronic disease and that there is no cure for it. RA can just be brought under control with medication. And usually the medication would last a lifetime. I was devastated. How the hell did I get this? Why me? And I felt that I was too young to get arthritis. How will I manage the rest of my life? So many questions unanswered.

The day I came to know about it, I was so depressed that I messaged Mohanji about the issue. He just replied – "Talk to Subhasree from London." I contacted Subhasree to know that even she was suffering from the same issue and had been on treatment for some time. She immediately called me, consoled and convinced me that things will turn for better with treatment, lifestyle change and of course supreme faith in the Guru. She guided me to a naturopathy treatment center in Kerala. At the same time, I consulted a Rheumatologist and started medication. He didn't give a definite timeline for the treatment and just said it might take long as it differs from person to person. The medication was also a low potency medicine given for cancer treatment. It had side effects like extreme hair fall. It was horrific to think that I might be bald soon!

Even after the medication, when the pain didn't subside, the doctor advised steroids. I was extremely scared of taking steroids. But at the same time, I didn't have another option either. At that moment I remembered an incident where Mohanji had mentioned to another devotee that if medication is needed, to take it, but offer and surrender to Mohanji, and he sees to it that it doesn't have any side effects. So before taking it, I just prayed to Mohanji to help me so it doesn't cause other side effects on my body other than what it is meant for. Finally, I also took 2 steroid injections. The pain subsided, but again after 3 months, I had to take another dose. By this time, I had started exploring other options of holistic treatments. I went for a 10 day detox in a naturopathy hospital in Kerala.

Meanwhile, going back in time, when the RA was first detected, in the first week, we had meditations in Preeti Duggal's house in Bangalore. After the meditations, we started speaking and I happened to mention to Preetiji about my RA condition. She gave one look at me and said, "I don't think it's got anything to do with physical ailment. This looks like more of an emotional issue which has erupted as this condition." She also advised me that I should go for Mai-Tri Method. At that time, I didn't know much about it. Since it was something that was given by Mohanji, I had complete faith that it would help. So I requested Preetiji to do Mai-Tri for me and booked an appointment with her.

The day came for the session, and Preetiji just asked me to lie down. Mohanji Gayathri was playing beautifully in the background. I knew Mohanji would take care, come what may. She started the process and we didn't talk much, but I could feel the heat in her hands while moving over the various chakra points of my body. I just surrendered completely to Mohanji and relaxed. After Mai-Tri, when I got up, I saw Preetiji sitting on the floor, as if she was handling something of high intensity or frequency, and almost shivering. She then slowly got up and came to the chair beside me. She started telling me what she saw during the Mai-Tri Method.

"First of all, your faith in Mohanji was so high, that you were completely open for Mohanji to work, for his energy to work. The receptivity and faith in you was so high that Mohanji's healing energy was at a high intensity. Since the energy was so high, I was not able to take it at one point, and I started shivering and had to sit down. Second, I saw that this pain is because of the trauma you are carrying from one of your previous lives, where you had a very abusive husband. In that life, you had been physically and mentally tortured to a great extent, and had died because of that torture. I could see that you still had bruises all over your body, and burnt marks like those made by cigarette butts on your body while you were dying. This was the trauma which was carried over lifetimes and it had manifested in this life in the form of this ailment. I could see Mohanji clearing the blockages in your body, and since you were so receptive, the energy was flowing beautifully through all your chakras."

I was in a state of shock. But it was what it was. Then I realised why Mohanji says never carry the memory or emotion of any particular incident. It gets stored in every cell of our body, and we even carry those emotions and memories over lifetimes. Since these memories become impressions, these impressions manifest in similar situations. When an issue happens, look at it objectively. If something has happened, if it's wrong, try to correct it. If it's an abusive relationship, and nothing can be done, move out. Do not take it passively. Instead, be objective enough to take action, or move out. This way we are not storing stuff. If you are feeling sad, cry it out, but then there is no need to store and lament over it for years. Mohanji says forgiveness of self and others, and acceptance are the biggest gifts you can give to yourself, and that is what the Power of Purity Meditation helps us to do.

With this one single Mai-Tri session, I could feel in the coming days, almost 60% of my symptoms of RA had come down. One of the days when I met Mohanji, I asked if I should get Mai-Tri done again. He said, "You should check with your practitioner and if need be get it done." I decided if one session can help so much, a couple more would help me clear this issue altogether. Meanwhile, I did various other alternative things. I also went to the Bosnian Pyramids with Mohanji and the Ravne Tunnels which is said to have healing energies. Upon return, I scheduled another appointment for a session of Mai-Tri with Milica from South Africa. By this time, I had already reduced my dosage of the medicines from twice a day to once a week.

Mai-Tri with Milica was another divine experience. Milica would tell me then and there as to the results of energising and healing each chakra in the body. She saw that Mohanji was healing me with a divine bright light, and a major blockage from the solar plexus region was removed by him. It looked like a huge black ball. She asked me if any of my grandmothers had a knee problem. I tried to recollect and realised that my paternal grandmother had knee pain and swelling for as long as I could remember. She had passed away a few years back though. She mentioned that I was carrying her pain and that is the reason I was still suffering those joint issues. She was hovering around me, and then Mohanji stepped in and healed my grandmother, and asked her if she needed anything else or was it ok if she be released from this plane? My grandmother said she wanted to be released. So Mohanji healed and released her to the divine white light. Oh my God!!!

I have learnt two things from all this. We carry our lineage karma, which includes physical ailments too. And with Mai-Tri, Mohanji is healing and helping the lineage also, just not us. How much more compassionate can one be! Aren't we supremely blessed, that Mohanji is not only releasing us from our miseries but also our ancestors from all this? My medication by this time had reduced to almost once in 15 days, or whenever I used to feel the pain.

After all this, it so happened that I applied for the Kailash pilgrimage. As we all know, Kailash is an ultimate journey for a person in this lifetime. We were given a set of instructions of physical and breathing exercises to do, to prepare ourselves for this tough journey. It was almost a month before Kailash, and yet I was not able to do any of these due to various reasons. Just 15 days before the journey, my son suddenly fell ill with a high fever. Later I came to know it was a viral infection. It so happened that after his viral attack, I happened to fall sick with the same thing, though something like this had never happened before. May be it was another form of test/cleansing for Kailash (which Mohanji confirmed in Nepal, en route to Kailash). I became very weak and developed rashes all over my body. Forget about exercises, I was not able to get up from my bed. At the same time, my RA suddenly flared up. My knees were suddenly swollen. My left foot was completely swollen. I was not able to wear my sandals. All this when I was about to embark on a physically demanding journey? I started my RA medicines again, and got back to twice a day dosage. In spite of taking the medicines continuously for 15 days, the swelling didn't subside. I was getting more and more anxious about doing the 52 km parikrama in Kailash. But somewhere internally, I knew if Shiva has called, he will take care of it. I don't have to worry. And I surrendered to his will. It could also happen that due to the cold weather this condition could get worse and out of hand. Finally, I kept all the medicines with me and just prayed that whatever happens, I would face it. His will is my will. Just being there would be good enough for me, even if I don't do the parikrama.

When we reached Nepal, we had a satsang with Mohanji in Kathmandu. During one of the breaks, when I went to prostrate to Mohanji, I told him about my condition. He said it was not just me; almost everyone was facing some issue or the other in their lives before coming to Kailash. He also mentioned that Kailash was not an easy journey. And this was all a part of the cleansing process. Setting foot on the land of Kailash itself needed a certain kind of eligibility, and not everyone could do it. So even if we were doing the journey by the grace of the Guru, we all had to go through the purification process, which we had all been going through for months.

I told him that I wanted to do the parikrama and asked him to help me with it. He just replied – "You will, why not?" That was just enough for me. I knew he will take care and I don't have to worry. It has been my previous experience with other Mohanji pilgrimages that although we are not completely physically fit for a demanding trek, in his energy and with complete surrender, we are different people altogether – highly energetic, no signs of fatigue, stress, strain, etc. It proved to be true in this trip too. Though we were in the coldest of regions with low levels of oxygen, I didn't have any signs of fatigue or any of the symptoms of RA. I even forgot to take my RA medicines, though I was carrying them along with me. That was the level of energy that we were in.

At Yamadwar, I prayed for liberation, and to let go of all that is not required for spiritual progress, be it physical, emotional, materialistic relations, things, etc. I did the entire parikrama, some on a pony and some on foot, without a single sign of weakness, breathlessness, or joint pain. Nothing! It was a breeze!! How powerful is our Guru and his grace? How compassionate and loving he is, in spite of all our misdoings, helping us sail through the toughest journey like it was child's play. When we have faith and surrender, Guru's grace will give us the toughness and the tenacity to go through any situation and that is what I experienced in this holy journey to Kailash.

When I came back home from the trip, I forgot all about the RA. I stopped taking the medications too. It's been 4 months now, and I have neither felt the signs of it till now nor have I felt the need to take medication. From impossible to possible is what Mohanji is all about. I am M-powered! No amount of words can convey my gratitude to the Guru and the Guru Mandala for showering me with so much grace, love and care. It was not only me, but even the lineage has also been healed.

I bow down with deep gratitude and surrender to all the Masters of the Guru Mandala and Mohanji for healing me from this impossible ailment and ridding me of it completely!!

Guru Leela

Grace that Heals

DIVINE CALL OF NATURE

Cathy Johnston, UK

Having gone through 30 years of various gynaecological procedures (and subsequent total hysterectomy 10 years ago) following the respective births of my two giant-sized babies (10 lb each), I had become used to living under the governance of my ever-increasing bladder alerts. Wherever I travelled I'd automatically, mentally calculate my liquid intake and the very real prospect of a cross-legged stagger to the nearest bush (in the face of a commonplace lack of public conveniences).

Most often, my decision was a toss-up between remaining hydrated, and taking the risk, or deciding to dehydrate to avoid a crisis. The latter usually prevailed. Day times weren't the only problem, this was a 24/7 vigil with sleep disturbances a 'normal' for me. Aeroplane and coach journeys were the things of nightmares. Careful consideration and planning beforehand were extremely necessary for me.

When the opportunity to attend Mohanji's Serbian retreat (October 2019) came up, the first considerations that came to mind were all of the above.

(A couple of months before the planning of the travel for the retreat, I had had the dawning that my next birthday would be the big six zero. I had then decided, once and for all, that the time was right to get my problem sorted before I began my 6th decade and duly made an appointment to visit a female gynaecologist in Manchester. Unsurprisingly, it was confirmed that I had a prolapsed bladder and required one of two surgeries. Another appointment – for the investigation to decide which one of the two operations I needed – was planned for the Wednesday after I'd arrive home from Mohanji's Serbian retreat.)

I have to admit I was sorely tempted not to attend with the thought of flying 2 hours to Zurich followed by a 5-hour coach ride (did it have an onboard loo?) was too much to contemplate. I was travelling with my younger son via a stop-over with him in Switzerland, and who, by sheer and ruthless pester-power (and a lack of real empathy or knowledge about the debilitating and restrictive condition I lived with) convinced me there would be a loo on board the coach and that all would be well.

Mentally, I decided I'd abstain from all liquid refreshments and be prepared to arrive at the retreat feeling like a prune. I could re-hydrate in the comfort of my room with my lovely private en-suite. (Just as well I'd planned ahead as there wasn't a loo on board the coach – we did, however, stop halfway at a service where I made 3 trips to their ladies room).

Before booking, I had also noted the 'code of conduct' sentence that prompted those who needed to leave the room regularly (speaking directly to me!) during satsang, would be best advised to sit at the rear of the hall to avoid interrupting Mohanji's flow, etc. The first satsang arrived during our first evening together with around 200 other attendees, so I made sure I arrived early to pick my seat at the back, not wanting to have to elbow other, like-bladdered women out of the way.

(Incidentally, all of this particular retreat's events/words/language was entirely alien to me – not to my son of course who had occasionally uttered these Indian sounding words in my presence – so my expectations were basically, zero!)

The evening of the first satsang arrived (satsang – what does this mean?), and I duly sat at the end of a back-row seat. Unfortunately, as fate would have it, the blonde lady in front of me had rather big, fuzzy hair and my views were so restricted that I found myself constantly bobbing up and down as I became more and more drawn to the truth this Mohanji person was speaking. I became very frustrated (also a little exhausted after such a long journey) but cannily spotted the next seat for the following day that I would nab. I'd get there early once again to avoid any drama!

The following day's satsang arrived with me smugly seated at the end of a curved middle row, close to another exit door. I settled in and was so happy with my perfect view. I'd monitored my liquid intake and knew I could last about an hour before having to 'nip to the loo'.

About halfway through, my mind became distracted by my usual obsession as I wondered when a good time would be to duck out invisibly, not wanting to draw attention to myself or disrupt the flow. I was also beginning to cross my legs and in all honesty, didn't want to miss a trick of what was going on. I was captivated by this person. He spoke to my own heart, directly, speaking my truth and reassuring me about myself. I was transfixed and also uncomfortable with the increasing knowledge of an imminent dash becoming quite necessary.

Suddenly, out of the blue, Mohanji stopped speaking and asked aloud 'does somebody need to go to the toilet?' My heart stopped and skipped a beat as I shrank down into my seat and averted my gaze, praying to God no-one would recognise my body language and realise it was me!! God only knows how I managed to sit through the next half of the satsang, but I was puzzled. I wondered, "Did this person read my mind? How can this be? This has to be a coincidence," blah blah, as I raced out at the end.

At some stage later that day, we all toddled off for our 'Conscious walking' session in the glorious sunshine on the beautiful Serbian mountainside. Sitting quietly on a rocky outcrop at our mountain top destination, my son and I were discussing the experience so far when I felt a gentle hand on my head as someone navigated the bumps of the hill around where we were sitting. I thought absolutely nothing of it and looked up and smiled at Mohanji as he gently ambled on with the group he was walking with.

My son, looking wide-eyed and directly at me, was gasping; "Mum, Mum, Mohanji has just blessed you! Do you realise what this means?" I was smiling but really, in total ignorance of the whole shaboodle so far. Nothing was normal to me. The whole experience so far was a million miles away from my everyday life. All of these people talking so freely about their emotions and problems and this wonderfully wise guy walking casually amongst us all. (I was trying really hard to process but as the days wore on, my mind was becoming more and more mushed.)

I can't remember the exact sequence of events but at some stage, we were informed that the timetable for the following day was to begin an hour earlier at 6 am and we were to go directly to the dining hall to drink a litre and a half of water followed by 12 almonds. Really? Why would this be? How was I going to cope with the two-hour yoga session afterwards? (In truth, yoga was the deciding factor for attending this retreat and if it hadn't been on the agenda, I definitely could have resisted the power of pestering!)

I was genuinely distraught, my body was craving for some yoga but I knew, deep down, that my whole week of yoga was in jeopardy with this ridiculous new instruction and the subsequent million dashes I'd have to make during yoga, in every session, disrupting the others, etc. and causing embarrassment to myself. Darn it! I felt that this week was going to be ruined for me and that I'd return home as unfit as I'd arrived.

The first session of yoga, following our new water and nut regime, was amazing. Yoga like I'd never experienced and from the word go, we were totally immersed in the feelings within. Starting with the gapless breathing (again something new for me) followed by the traditional full-body workout yoga session.

I hadn't anticipated the overwhelming emotions at the commencement of 'Shavasana' when a wonderful guitar sprang to life and the most mournful voice began to sing its tune. I was unsure if this was a live or recorded performance and longed to know if it was live.

Upon rousing, I saw it was the beautiful Natesh, but my taps by this time were already on full-flow and thankfully, from my eyes. I couldn't control my sorrowful weeping and was very confused as to what was happening to me. (Luckily, my Son was there to console me but I was growing more and more puzzled with all of these new sensations and feelings that were overwhelming me.)

The following day was almost the same, if not, more tears and it was only during the second half of this second day, during the afternoon, that it suddenly dawned on me that 'Hold on! What's going on here? I haven't been dashing out to the loo, this can't be right, I've seen so many people nipping in and out of the yoga sessions and not ONCE have I had to leave the room, this is bizarre, maybe I have soaked up all of the water because of the long dehydrating journey?'

I tried hard to fathom it all and maybe, after the 3rd day, I began to mention this to some of the other women I had made friends with. Each one of them smiled knowingly, some even giggled and I was dumbfounded. 'How could anyone heal someone else's bladder without surgery? What is happening to me? Who is this person?'

Words are so feeble a tool to try to convey the atmosphere during this event and I kept thinking to myself; 'being here is believing, there are no words adequate enough to encapsulate the feelings and emotions bubbling up so frequently unannounced'.

More and more, I had the overwhelming feeling that I was witnessing something truly sacred and divine and I felt genuinely humbled to be enveloped by the grace of this person and his beautifully natural and unassuming family.

One particular word (Mohanji used more often than any other) tickled me and brought to mind a Beatles tune 'All you need is Love'. It was Mohanji's pronunciation of the English word, 'Love' that sounded like 'low' which made me smile every time he spoke it and this tune became cemented, on a permanent loop within my mind.

I became convinced throughout the remainder of the retreat that I had been touched by the grace of God and had even had a flesh-hug from the same. How could I possibly explain this to the people back home? Where would I begin to describe the goings-on and wonderfulness of it all? I then began to dread the prospect of being without these people, this new, spiritual family I had found.

I also had the prospect of my second gynaecological exploratory appointment looming on the

Wednesday after my return home at the weekend. 'Would it be prudent to go along? Would this be an insult to Mohanji and maybe reverse my 'miracle cure?' What was I to do? Who would know the answer? Would attending this second consultation back home cast doubt upon my faith?' I was in a quandary and towards the last day, I began to ask the advice of one or two people. My son was adamant and quite assertive in that I had to keep my faith and cancel the consultant's appointment. Someone else told me the answer was within me. Turmoil!

The final evening dawned and it was my time to have a one to one, 3 minutes with Mohanji. I was more troubled with thoughts about my elder son and his future life and the recent near-fatal accident of my husband to think about using these precious minutes to ask about my personal, troubling decision. So I nervously blathered on to Mohanji about my husband and our life of striving together, ignoring the 'Elephant in the room' question.

After Mohanji had delivered his reassurances regarding my spoken troubles, I thanked him but just as I was about to open the door to leave him, I turned around and asked him outright, "Did you heal my bladder?" to which he responded, in his gentle, half-smiling way, **"I am always at work."**

My journey homeward bound was to stay two nights with my son in Switzerland, before flying back to the UK. During the first day out in Switzerland, I was dismayed to notice a slight return in my need to find the nearest ladies' room and on my return to

Geneva airport for my trip back to the UK, I glumly noted the frequency was increasing.

My 21:30 flight was delayed by two hours which meant a dismal hanging around a half-empty airport and once past security I found myself dashing towards the nearest loo. Typical of my pre-Mohanji cure, once inside the cubicle I had a frantic dash to prevent an accident and I felt utterly despondent and really confused as to all that had just occurred, in the space of a week. Did my indecision to cancel my consultant's upcoming appointment reveal my lack of faith and put doubt into my mind regarding the healing?

I was at a complete and utter loss, with no-one to help or support me, so I looked up from the cubicle and asked Mohanji out loud, "Please Mohanji, tell me what to do, am I being punished for doubting or lacking in faith and by keeping my appointment will this undo all of the work you have done? Please help me." I was feeling very sad and unhappy and so unsure of myself and the decision I had to make.

As I walked towards the washbasin and pressed for the soap, I looked into the mirror and suddenly noted that the song coming from the piped music was none other than 'All you need is Love!' I literally laughed out loud and smiled at myself and spoke out loud to Mohanji in complete and utter thanks.

My answer had arrived, and he'd known all along that I had had that tune in my head, throughout the whole week. How funny! God has got a great sense of humour and does work in the most surprising ways.

Needless to say, I duly cancelled my consultant's appointment for the Wednesday ahead and have never looked back (or have had to keep my eyes peeled for the nearest convenience!).

Once again, words cannot begin to convey my gratitude for the whole, surreal and ultimately, humbling experience but most of all for my reintroduction to the God within. Mohanji, (I'm smiling now, typing his name) the world will indeed be healed. All we need is Love.

To share my wonderful experiences with my nearest and dearest was really difficult (as I had anticipated) but the worst for me was not confiding in my Mum. My mum is undeniably my best friend; she's clever, funny, has a wicked sense of humour and has always shared my every significant moment. The opportunity arrived when she came for an extended visit last week. I bravely printed off my testimonial and handed it to her. (Did I forget to say she's an atheist?). I left the room to let her absorb the info and came back in, sat down beside her, looked her straight in the eye and asked her, "What do you think mum?"

She was very quiet, looked right into my eyes and said, "It's very strange, but do you know something funny, my bladder problems have stopped too!"

I vaguely recall Henry (the younger son who dragged me to Serbia) mentioning the fact that once we are blessed by Mohanji then our whole family would be blessed too. So I sketchily mentioned this to my Mum. She responded with a bewildered look in her eyes and an audible 'Mmmmm', so I left it at that. Later on, yesterday, I heard from the lovely Owen and after telling him this story, he explained the lineage facts which became so much clearer to me (having had this whole experience) and my jaw literally dropped.

My maternal grandmother had the same bladder issues and so the story ends with my cure!

I'm so giddy with this new knowledge and living day proof (from a hard-wired skeptic too!) that I want to share it with the whole world.

I was so happy going to bed last night and asked Mohanji if he could help me sleep without me having to take a melatonin (a long boring story of years of debilitating insomnia and the wonderful melatonin solution I discovered this year). I boldly left the tablet to one side knowing I'd be heard by Mohanji. My husband followed me to bed and immediately about turned to sleep in the spare room when he heard my melodious snores. I had the most wonderfully deep and restful sleep since I can remember and I can't wait to see if my mum did too!

Thank you Mohanji for your care and connection with/for us. I asked and you delivered and my faith has been rewarded yet again. Please let your grace be available to everyone through the vehicles of us all.

"RISE"
Above moments into eternity
Above emotions into devotion
Above time into timelessness
Above suffering into acceptance
Above mind into liberation.

*Live your life based on your own truth,
as you experienced it.
When you live your own truth
moment to moment,
you are stable, irrespective of
fluctuations - the rises and falls of life.*

A FRIEND FOR LIFE

A devotee, India

I am a believer of 'karma' and have always tried to 'do good' and 'be good'. Worshipping idols was something that came to me only as a ritual, instilled by family. I had never believed in the concept of a 'Guru' in human form and I would like to attribute this belief to my childhood experiences of a human Guru, who was revered by my parents, and many of our acquaintances. My parents could never convince me to revere him. By the grace of God, my instincts didn't fail me and I did not have to experience what others did. That chapter closed when he left this earthly abode. My regards stay with him for sparing us.

At the age of 44, I was caught in a whirlwind of depression attack, a very severe one at that. Frankly speaking, my husband and I were ignorant about the implications of depression, its cause and consequences, till my condition worsened so much that I had to be taken for a medical examination and was diagnosed with depression. What caused it; I still don't know quite well. Maybe it was an amalgamation of hormonal imbalance, the stress of taking life too seriously, striving to be perfect, and more so, expecting others to be perfect.

God has showered his grace on me many times, has bailed me out of many tough situations, and this time was no different. My then new neighbour, and now a bosom friend, guide and mentor, had taken pity on my depressive state and had given

Mohanji's eye-card to me. I would have preferred to, but actually couldn't say no to an ardent request made by her to look into those eyes (courtesy my childhood experience mentioned above). But, when life shoves you into a ditch, whether you like it or not, you want to bounce out of it by any means.

After I recovered, I was lucky to get a chance to meet him for the first time in 2015, in South India, at a satsang. I cannot frame in words the overwhelming feeling of being in the presence of someone who I had not met before, not spoken to, yet something within was churning and swelling tears, without any reason. I was warned by my friend that something like this may happen and I had internally laughed it out. But, I had wet so many tissues that day!

It's been 4 years since grace started flowing through those eyes and it continues. I started believing and revering Mohanji at the very instant I bounced back to life, but the mind as always sowed a seed of doubt – for me, it was – 'Really Mohanji or the medicines that worked?'

I even bothered him by asking, "How do I know who you are?" He had said, "You will know tonight." He came in my dream, showing his back to me like a dark silhouette, but showing me the face of Shirdi Sai Baba. I remember this so distinctly.

Barely 6 months after having recovered from the first attack, I suffered another attack the following year. I had happened to meet Mohanji again, at the end of the second depressive state. I had asked him, "Why again?" To which he replied, "You will get another attack next year." I was shattered to hear that! I had missed hearing the more important part, heard by the others in the room that, it would be mild and it would be my final clearing. And so it was! It came back again, it was mild and I managed to do my daily chores, with a certain amount of difficulty, but, not like the previous two episodes, wherein, I was left handicapped in all possible ways.

Guru walks into one's life when the disciple is ready and needs him the most - so I have read in Mohanji's blogs. This holds so true in my case and to many others who have known Mohanji.

Many address him as 'Father', but he has been like a friend to me – joking, cajoling, and explaining life like a story. No serious business! He opens his arms and takes anyone in his embrace and knows who is asking for what! To quote a few examples, here I go...

Knowing that I am not consistent with my spiritual practices, he has worked on me and made me do all the practices, through my friend acting as the conduit of energy flow. She remained as my neighbour for three years, till I recovered completely, and has now shifted away. I take it as a sign that I am now fine; hence the conduit has been withdrawn from proximity.

Mohanji graces many households with his footsteps and I have always wished the same for my household. Since the likelihood of physical footsteps is bleak, he appeared in my meditative state, sitting right in front of me on the sofa, and later merged into the frame of Sai Baba, which I have in my drawing-room.

I have seen him as tall as a mountain while taking a dip in the hot spring in Badrinath. He has appeared when I prayed for my mother-in-law, who was hospitalised with severe Parkinson's disorder and hallucinations. She has miraculously recovered to take care of herself.

Very recently, I got a chance to meet him at the consecration ceremony of a Sai Temple, by a Mohanji disciple in South India. While Mohanji was standing near the homam and was flanked by people all around, I had shut my eyes and was silently sending prayers to him to help a school friend of mine, who had misunderstood me and was going through a lot in her personal life. Tears had started to roll down my eyes when my friend patted me on the back and directed me to look at Mohanji, as he wanted me to look at him. He smiled at me in acknowledgement and I was left smiling back at him. I immediately realised it was a signal that he had heard my prayers!

My friend is now a trained Mai-Tri practitioner and she continues to guide me and clear me with Mohanji's energy. There are many instances wherein I have felt his presence and grace. I have now come to believe that suffering is a sign of clearance of past baggage and that there is sunshine behind the clouds. Guru helps to speed up the process. My heartfelt gratitude to Mohanji for coming into my life at a time of great need, offering unconditional love, healing and protection.

AN EXTENDED LEASE
A devotee, UK

I identify myself as someone who is deeply connected to Skanda Vale and Mohanji. I don't distinguish between them both, for me simply; the differences are the differences between a mother and father, or the left and right eyes. Since connecting to Mohanji, quite a lot of positive changes have happened in my personal and professional lives, simply because of a major transformation within me. Yes, my acceptance level has increased significantly with Mohanji's grace and I handle many situations that would upset a typical human being with ease. In general, my level of detachment has also increased day by day, so I find navigating through life relatively easy.

In early 2019, I had lost quite a lot of weight and all my friends and family asked me the reason behind it. I was also experiencing night chills and fatigue, but I was feeling very positive and was not bothered about it, getting on with my daily life as usual. I was not aware of a big test coming my way at that time.

Following Maha Shivarathri, I was briefly ill and went to see my GP (family doctor). The GP suspected a possible urinary tract infection and prescribed some antibiotics and ordered some tests. After a week, the test results came without any indication for infections, so she referred me to a urology consultant under a fast track arrangement. I was still not worried at all and went to see the consultant happily, hoping that everything would be fine.

He examined and reassured me that there was nothing to worry, but suggested some tests including a CT scan, and a procedure to send a camera inside the bladder (cystoscopy) to identify any potential issues. I was very positive as usual and drove to the hospital for the test on Friday the 15th of March, without expecting the shocking news that awaited me. The cystoscopy showed a tumour in my bladder. He said that from previous experiences it was 'almost certainly cancerous' and we should remove it as soon as possible, and see how far it had spread. He added that it appeared to be at an early stage, but he could only confirm further details after the surgery.

This was indeed very distressing for me. The face of my wife and two young children (one as young as 3 months old) came to my mind. I was shocked, didn't know what to do, but drove back home and shared the news with my wife. The next step I did was the stepping stone for me to write this story now. I sent an email to the Skanda Vale Swamis and also a message to a close friend who had introduced me to Mohanji and requested him to convey this news to Mohanji on my behalf. I collapsed emotionally, crying for no reason, and felt very low.

On the following day (16th), it happened to be a full moon weekend and we decided to go to the Divine Mother's full moon puja in Skanda Vale. On arrival, the Swamis asked me to come and sit in the front row and they all made a 'Sankalp' (intention) that Divine Mother's energy should heal me. In her hand, she carries a Lingam and in situations like this, the Swamis would bless the sick person with that Lingam. I was aware that this Lingam was materialised in the mid-80s, during meditation in Skanda Vale, from the divine hand of late Swami Premananda as a healing Lingam. Since then this Lingam has been in the Divine Mother's hand, and only during full moon Maha abishekams, the Swamis take it from her hand and bless the needy people. I have heard about many healing stories related to this Lingam and met a few people who have been healed by its divine power and energy.

As far as I understand, it is not something that we can request to have but comes our way if we are eligible. On that day, the Swami who led the puja took that Lingam and placed it on my forehead (third eye) and the top of the head (sahasra) and blessed me. I felt immense energy during the blessing. Once the blessing was finished, he immersed the Lingam in a bowl of milk and I saw the milk bubbling up immediately as if it was boiling. At this point, I said to myself, if my lease is extended and I come out of this, I would dedicate the rest of my life to serve the world. After the blessing and having handed over my burden to the Divine Mother, I came back home feeling very relieved.

When I arrived home, I saw that my friend had forwarded me a message from Mohanji. It read, **"I am with him, I am reducing its intensity. Feed the birds, fishes and animals, and do annadaan. I am with him."** Seeing this message was immensely reassuring for me. I immediately started feeding birds, like a sadhana, most days before my breakfast. I also started to carry some wild bird feed in my car, so that I could feed birds wherever I found them. After a while, I started to enjoy feeding and watching them.

I was beginning to feel a little relaxed after receiving both, blessings from Skanda Vale and Mohanji's comforting message. I had shared the news with some of my close friends within the Mohanji family. Needless to say, they were all shocked as well. However, two of them decided to come to my place (I live far away from many of the Mohanji family members) and did Mai-Tri many times. I received the first Mai-Tri on Tuesday the 19th of March. I had had my CT scan completed by this time, which confirmed the tumour, but showed that it hadn't spread to other parts of the body.

My consultant had scheduled the surgery for the 30th of March. I went to the hospital chanting the Mohanji Gayatri. While in the operation theatre, I closed my eyes and continued to chant after speaking with the anaesthetist. When I was back on the ward after the operation, I realised that I had gone under sedation chanting the Mohanji Gayatri. In the afternoon, the consultant visited me and confirmed that he had successfully removed a tumour which was 3 cm in size. He further said it appeared to him as typical early-stage bladder cancer, but he could only confirm and decide the treatment plan after the biopsy analysis.

I came home and struggled with post-operative recovery. Two of my friends from the Mohanji family came back again and did Mai-Tri. At the beginning of one of the healing sessions, the practitioner came towards me, went back a couple of steps, and then came back near me again. At the end of the session, he had something to reveal. He said, "When I came near, I couldn't see you, but Mohanji was sleeping on the bed. I couldn't believe it and was confused as to how I was going to do Mai-Tri to Mohanji, but then he said go ahead and do the healing, so I came back. You have nothing to worry; he is taking care of you." I was shocked to hear this and wondered if I was eligible for such grace. It was indeed a reconfirmation that Mohanji always does what he says, he was with me!

I had another revelation the next day. Mohanji was in Peru at that time and was suffering from some breathing difficulties and other illness on the same day that I had Mai-Tri. This was circulated in one of the Mohanji WhatsApp groups, and I started crying out of gratitude reading this news. I strongly felt that he was taking on my pain and was suffering as a result.

I had my follow-up appointment with my consultant, 3 weeks after surgery. The results of the biopsy were available by this time. The first thing my consultant said was, "You have to thank God. The results came as non-conclusive; the pathologist could not make a firm conclusion between a very rare benign tumour and early-stage cancer. The benign case is extremely rare with a probability of less than one in a hundred, so we should assume this as cancerous and plan accordingly. The good news is that it appears very superficial and has not invaded into the muscles yet. It's contained within the superficial tissue layer which is a surprise for me based on its size and the symptoms you have had (losing weight, fatigue, night chills and blood in the urine). You don't need any medication or further treatment unless it returns, so I recommend follow-up tests in 3 months and 1 year, and take it from there."

I came home very much relieved and full of gratitude to Skanda Vale and Mohanji for healing me. According to my understanding, a cancerous tumour had been transformed into a benign one, which made the pathologist confused, because the tumour was expressing both patterns. I immediately sent a message of gratitude to Mohanji through my friend. I also went to Skanda Vale the following weekend and thanked the Divine Mother and the community.

After a couple of months, I had attended a retreat with Mohanji. It was one of the bigger retreats with around 100 people in attendance. On the first instance, Mohanji called me by my first name and asked me, "How is your health?" I was pleasantly surprised to know that he remembered my name (Mohanji has thousands of followers in the world, and I am one of them, so I was not expecting him to remember my name and other details). It was another reassurance for me that he meant what he said, **"I am with him."**

A month after the retreat, I had my third-month follow-up with the consultant who confirmed that no abnormalities were found but recommended another test in 9 months to make sure the tumour had not returned. I sent a message to Mohanji through my friend, and he replied almost instantly with the following message. **"Please tell him to get Mai-Tri."** I immediately contacted one of the Mai-Tri practitioners who does distant Mai-Tri and had a session one night. At some point during the session, I felt like someone was pressing hard on the top of my head. After the session, the practitioner shared that she saw a silver-coloured snake protecting me around my head, and at one point blessed me by pressing its wide hood on me. She further said that she could see some dark spots like a cloud above my stomach area but there was a silver lining across it, and it had cleared by the end of the session. This was indeed another reassurance for me that the Tradition was looking after me.

Time passed quickly and I have had my first year check up on the 29th of January 2020. The consultant completed the cystoscopy and said, "Everything is 100% normal, we have nothing to do, I don't think I need to see you anymore, so I am signing you off!"

I can only say, "Thank you, Divine Mother, and thank you Mohanji." My life in the past year is yet another confirmation that grace can heal if we surrender completely.

Now I am enjoying an extended lease, because of my mother (Skanda Vale) and father (Mohanji), so I dedicate this life to serve the world to the best of my ability.

HEALING TOUCH

Elham Khordadian, USA

Before the Acharya training in Serbia, many miracles took place in my life. However, the miracles during the training were very clear and eminent. I could see how Mohanji was removing my karma and that of others. He also removed the karma between all the Acharyas in the training. Lots of things were going on in my body. After the first few days, I got a very severe infection in my throat with many blisters. I was completely aware that he was cleansing me and he confirmed it too. My throat had big blockages for many years and one of the signs of the blockages was Hashimoto Hypothyroid, for which I was on medication for twenty years. It was no surprise that in every retreat, I was with Mohanji, my throat would get infected during or at the end of the program. But this time, all the clearing processes were accelerated and my throat was clear after two or three days. Usually, it would last for 7-10 days.

On the last night of the training, when I had an experience of Mother Kundalini by his grace, Mohanji came to me and with his fingers, pressed my throat. I felt a huge and heavy blockage being removed and energy started flowing with pressure in my body. It was like removing a dam from the way of a river. After that night, I heard in my heart that I don't need medication anymore. The message was so clear and loud! I immediately stopped the medications without even checking with my doctor because I had complete faith that Mohanji had removed the problem with my throat. It's been three months now since I stopped the medication and I feel much more energized and healthy. It's only because of his grace and blessings and there are no words to express my gratitude to him. This body, mind, intellect, ego and spirit are at the lotus feet of my Baba Mohanji.

ON HEALING AND LETTING GO

Hein Adamson, India

I had an appointment with Milica for a session of the Mai-Tri Method of deep cleansing, harmonising and healing. I was early and everyone was out, so I had a few minutes to myself. I could feel that something big might be on its way. I decided to visit the altar while I waited for everyone. Devotion and deep, uninterrupted connectivity to the Mohanji consciousness have transformed Milica's house into a temple. I prostrated and sat before the altar, feeling. Only sitting and feeling; Mohanji's presence so palpable, stillness descends. This is my Father's house. Wherever a true disciple lives, there too, lives the Master. Without Mohanji's blessing I would not have been able to enter, he had brought me here to receive something profound, through her. Whenever I am forgetful of my path and my purpose, Mohanji ensures that I am reminded.

As we started to prepare for Mai-Tri, we were talking, as we usually do, about Mohanji, and our respective journey and understandings. I really enjoy speaking with people like her because rarely will she ever speak unless what is being spoken about is something which has been deeply felt, to the very core, which is alive and vivid. Truth spoken from the depths is rich and spontaneous.

The Mai-Tri session opened with an invocation, "If it is karmically correct, let this person be healed by Mohanji." I thought to myself that whatever happens if I am to derive any benefit, I must be as open as possible, I must receive every last drop that I am capable of receiving. This was a very important decision. As the session progressed, I felt the intimacy and vulnerability of the situation; I knew that in my innermost chambers. I felt safe, but the recoil was instinctive, so I had to continually tell myself to stay open, to be vulnerable and it paid off!

The practitioner's hands are placed at different energy centres in the body and at one point, as her hands were on my heart centre; I saw that Milica's hands weren't hers at all, but Mohanji's! I've spent a lot of time staring at Mohanji's hands, I know what they look like and there can be no mistake. The image was so clear, the practitioner had disappeared entirely and it was Mohanji standing next to me as I lay, his hands on my heart. He wore white, the colour which represents purity, and the path of liberation. I know that Mohanji loves us, I 'know'... But I had never imagined such tenderness as that which flowed from those hands; never experienced such love. Love so vast that when it enters, there is no room left in you for anything else. How could I possibly have deserved to feel such a thing? It is impossible to earn such love. It is only given. It can only be the nature of the giver.

Along with this came guidance, information that I desperately needed. "Do you feel dead inside?" She asked me. "Yes", I answered. Some weeks prior, finding myself in a particularly self-confrontational situation, I suddenly felt a deadness within, as if all of my insides were made from great slabs of dead meat like a carcass hung up to drain after slaughter. I even remember the moment it came to me, stopping me where I stood. It was a terrible, paralysing feeling. "You have been carrying this with you for many, many lives." The session progressed. "You are cutting yourself off from others, you feel that it is better to be alone, but it is a mask." This was familiar to me, but I had always thought that the tendency towards solitude is a positive thing, a sign of detachment. Not so in this case. "You have also been carrying great fear for many lives." So on it went...

Afterwards, we discussed all the things which had come up. There was an idol of Shirdi Sai Baba in the room with us, in front of which was placed a small candle. The wick had split and the little flame was burning very strongly. I was told it was a sign of how many lifetimes of garbage had been removed. A great revelation that I had through this session was that I had been carrying things with me over a great many lives, things which I needn't have carried at all. I clung on to them for no good reason; life afterlife, weighing myself down, feeding the heaviness and the deadness and the fear. Unnecessary suffering! By Mohanji's grace, these can all be let go of.

"You didn't come here to perpetuate these patterns; you came to finish them off. Connect more with Mohanji, read the blogs, watch the YouTube videos. The more you connect, the lighter you will become" was the parting message.

It has been about 3 days since this happened and even now I can feel huge changes as if the entire inner landscape is being turned over and rearranged. I feel lighter, I feel Mohanji more, I can catch myself disconnecting from his consciousness and correct it. I feel a hope and optimism I haven't felt in years. My mind is still hustling and bustling, but I am a little further away from it, there is a little more space and stillness within.

Ever in gratitude, and surrendered at Mohanji's feet.

GLIMPSES OF MIRACLES

Ivana Kodzic, Serbia

I would like to share a few experiences, which I had during my practices as a Mohanji Transformation Method (MTM) practitioner. As an MTM practitioner, I get to see Mohanji working in various dimensions. This is a technique where I connect to him and he works through me on the subtle bodies of individual clients by removing the root cause of their issues. I remember a few cases that were very inspiring and transformative. Sometimes the change comes over time and sometimes there is an instant change, such as saving lives.

One such case happened last year when a client messaged me one evening. She was my client from before. She had some issues with her boyfriend and she was supposed to get married to him. On the day when she was supposed to pick up her wedding dress, she was suddenly fed up with the abusive relationship she was in, and she decided that it was enough.

She explained to him over the phone that she hadn't picked up the dress because she didn't want to get married. He then got into such a rage that he threatened to kill her and was willing to end up in jail. She recorded the 15 minutes message and sent it to me. I have never felt such fear in my life because from the guy's voice it was so clear that he was seriously on his way to kill her. Luckily, he was not anywhere near. He was travelling from another country and he was on his way to kill her. She was very afraid and she messaged me in panic, feeling scared for her life.

First of all, I felt fear myself. And it was something that doesn't happen. Usually, whatever people say to me, during the sessions or whenever they ask for help, I stay stable and I don't feel fear in those moments. But this time fear was building up more and more and I didn't know what to do. I started to panic myself and asked Mohanji what to do. I heard him saying it is not your fear, now sit and work.

I realised at that moment that I had tapped into the energy of fear which belonged to her and had I picked up some of that energy. He also explained that at the moment when she was releasing her fear, it was also directing the killer's energy inside of him. So, these two energies combined were feeding each other. It was not good for her to experience fear. So Mohanji pulled it out through me.

As I calmed down after a few minutes, I sat down and started to do this session. Mohanji showed me that there was a repetitive pattern between the two of them, of victim and victimizer, and there was abuse and killing even in their past lives. It would repeat itself in this life as well if Mohanji didn't intervene.

Mohanji also showed me in this situation that her decision to get married was a product of a vow which was given in one of their previous lives.

So in an earlier life, she had sworn that she will get married to him. When we give such vows in some life, we don't realise that this will follow us in future incarnations as well. So, he released that vow as well, released her fear, and plucked out the root cause of the issue, which was embedded from previous lives.

Meanwhile, I was aware of Mohanji working on that guy as well. I had a vision of him driving the car in rage and there was energy working through him. He was a drug addict and he attracted various dark energies with his way of life. So he was not himself. While he was driving, Mohanji was working on him and changed his mind, releasing these negative energies as well and calming him down. The result was that he didn't make it to her at all. I don't remember the reason, but he didn't come to her at all.

Even though she was not connected to Mohanji from before, and she had only heard of him through me, she could feel that he had saved her life and she was very grateful. She was completely aware of the shift in her destiny, and she was grateful that she didn't end up murdered.

It is sometimes the case that clients are not even aware of what Mohanji did for them. I'm also not allowed to share in such cases because neither Mohanji nor the Tradition wants people to follow or to connect to Mohanji only because they know that he saved their lives. He wants them to follow and connect from the heart, because he feels it is the right thing for them to do as it leads them to liberation, to happiness, and a meaningful and stress-free life.

So, even in such cases, I'm not always allowed to share, unless the clients feel that there was a great shift that happened and they experienced it. This was the case with this girl so I could share with her what actually could have happened to her. That is the miracle of how Mohanji saved her life and how he works in so many dimensions simultaneously. We see him in physical reality, sitting, talking or reading something on his phone, but we are not aware of where he's working at that moment or in which dimension. I can see that various dimensions are simultaneously happening at the same time. While he's sitting, I can see him working on so many people, helping them, saving them.

One of these cases of saving lives happened in my family as well. When my sister gave birth to her first child, I repetitively saw one vision. Their baby was a year, year and a half old and she was running through the house. I was visiting them at that time in Norway and I saw myself sitting, and while the child was running around, yelling 'aunty', suddenly she falls. She injures her head with a lot of blood of oozing out. We rush her to the hospital and my sister is panicking and that is where the vision would stop. This vision kept repeating several times. So I got a bit worried and asked Mohanji why he keeps showing me that vision. At that moment, I realised that I completely forgot that even with people who are close to him, or people who are aware of certain things, he doesn't interfere with their karma. So he showed me the vision. And he intervenes only when I request for help in the form of a prayer. So I prayed to him for help in that case.

That day did arrive. And I remember experiencing in reality, something that I saw in the vision, but this time, the result was completely different. She was running around calling me and she fell, but she didn't even get a scratch on her forehead.

Later on, when we were at Kumbh Mela, I spoke to him about that. He just looked at me and said, "Permanent disability." So that was the outcome of the first scenario that was possible for her. And I was completely aware of how he changed, literally changed her life. And I cannot express my gratitude enough for what he did for my family and what he keeps doing for other people.

As a Mohanji Transformation Method practitioner, I get to see many of these transformations, but I also get to see how people are sometimes ignorant or even take these things for granted. Even when they are aware that the possibility was high for them to experience something very unpleasant, or even that their lives were threatened and they were saved only by Mohanji, after some time, they just forget it. And that I guess is unfortunately inherent in human beings.

I remember a case about a lady living abroad who used to represent her country in sports. She called me complaining about severe pain in her hip. And she told me that doctors didn't know what was going on with her because she was very fit, being into sports all her life. She was very fit and healthy, and suddenly her hips started to fall apart with too much pain and they even scheduled surgery within the next two weeks. So when I did the session, Mohanji showed me that the spirit of her grandfather was in her, causing pain in her hip. The grandfather had had hip problems himself. It was a case of how spirits can give symptoms of diseases that they had while they were in the physical body. Mohanji released this spirit and healed him. For a few days, I didn't hear back from this lady, but then I heard that she had completely recovered and there was no need for surgery. It was so amazing to witness this miracle!

For me, it is always a blessing to see how Mohanji works with spirits and other energies because he's so gentle and helpful to these lost constitutions as well. In some practices, I've seen that people who release spirits send the spirit from within a person to an animal or some other object. But when he works, he releases the spirits and heals them. This process helps these souls to not carry these impressions from their previous lives to their next incarnation. So in this case, it was obvious that not just the person in physical reality was helped by saving her from surgery and so much pain, but also the soul who left would not have to incarnate with hip problems in the next life. This is the grace of a Master.

It is always interesting to see how Mohanji works constantly. Whenever I'm sitting with him in physical reality, I am aware of all that is happening in the room. Even when he is sitting with several people and they are talking amongst themselves, something is happening. He's looking at his phone but on some other level, work is getting done. Something is always happening and nothing is a coincidence. We may think something is healed or released only in his physical presence because we only see what is going on in that room; what about all the other rooms around the world which he is covering simultaneously. This happens only when someone has the energy of the Source itself. It doesn't drain him, it doesn't affect him.

In the beginning, I used to think why am I bothering him by asking so many questions astrally? I used to feel I'm disturbing him when he's doing something else. And then I realised that he doesn't have a beginning and he doesn't have an end, and he is the Source himself. He's omnipresent and he's available to everyone all the time, whenever we seek his help. Whenever we need help or guidance, he's there for us.

As Mohanji is pure light, he dispels the darkness. And it is so touching and so beautiful to see how he works so selflessly and even knowing that people will not know or appreciate what he does. And not even valuing whether it's someone close to him, or someone who is there for the first time, he keeps giving and helps everyone equally without expecting anything in return. And this is how he always does his job. He always tells me, "I do my job." And that is something that I've witnessed so many times. I feel so blessed and grateful that he has shown me these dimensions of his, and once he told me I have shown you almost everything. But I know that even these glimpses which I saw are just one tiny part of what he's doing. And I don't think while in the body, we can comprehend or to understand how he works, but then with this limited awareness, I can say that it is a lot. My sincere hope is that one day; he will at least be understood and appreciated for what he's been doing so selflessly.

Guru Leela

MOHANJI AND MY MOTHER

Jyoti Bahl, India

A Guru is comparable to the Sun; he spreads the light of liberation to all who seek it. Anyone who comes into his presence can benefit from it. A Guru is the face of God. Your real Guru is God Himself. He is the power who guides your spiritual efforts. He is always with you as your true self and your inner witness. To have Mohanji as our Sathguru is definitely because of good karma from previous lives. He does so much for all of us and we selfish humans forget everything. My life is full of Baba Sai's and Mohanji's experiences. It's all because of Baba Sai that I have Mohanji as my Guru. Since Mohanji entered my life, I don't feel lonely as I feel him every moment. It's not only a feeling, but he also proves his presence to me whenever I feel helpless, or when I'm in a bad situation. Since I have known him, Mohanji has saved the lives of my father, son, and even me! How can I define the glory of my Gurudev, who is like the vast ocean?

In 2019, Mohanji gave me many indications personally and through dreams about the problem which was coming up in my life. In March 2019, I was able to meet Mohanji. That meeting was truly blissful as I got the chance to listen to Bhaja Govindam by Sri Jagatguru Adi Shankaracharya, in Mohanji's powerful voice. Bhaja Govindam contains the essence of Vedanta, and implores man to think, why am I here in this life? Why am I gathering wealth and family, but have no peace? What is the truth? What is the purpose of life? The person who is awakened gets set on a path back to the God Principle. While listening to this bhajan in Mohanji's voice, I was in tears. I didn't want to come out of that blissful moment. The translation of every verse given by Mohanji was going into each cell of mine. I later realised the reason why I was singing these verses. Mohanji told me about detachment through Bhaja Govindam. At the end of March, my mother was detected with fourth stage cancer, which was no less than a nightmare for all of us. Before this, I used to have dreams about Mohanji very often, in which he used to call mother near him to bless her. These dreams started in Jan 2019. For the last few months, my mother had wanted to meet Mohanji, but it hadn't been possible due to some reason or the other.

I used to tell my mother about my astral meetings with him. I met Mohanji at the end of March and in the same month, got a chance to visit Shirdi as well. After I came back from Shirdi, I got to know about my mother's condition. And then I felt the power of Sathguru Mohanji, as he gave me so much strength to deal with a problem which was next to impossible for an ordinary person like me. With his motivation, I was prepared to give my mother quality time as all the doctors told us that her fourth stage cancer was not curable.

Mohanji asked me to contact a particular doctor and also gave me Lord Dattatreya's healing mantra for my mother. From the very first day, Mohanji sent Dr Harpreet Wasir into our lives, and he guided us at every step related to my mother's health. Many doctors were suggesting chemo. But I didn't want my mother to go through it as she had always been a very lively person. One day in my prayers, I surrendered to Baba Sai and Mohanji completely and within a few minutes, I got a call from Dr Wasir saying that mother need not go for chemo and he also added that let the doctors say anything. I was in such peace after listening to him. Just as I was praying to Mohanji for the same thing, Baba gave a message to one of my friends that my mother's life expectancy was very short, and we just have to give maximum love to the soul.

My mother's first amazing experience was when she went for a PET scan. She was a little scared during the test so she closed her eyes and called out to Mohanji. Within seconds, Mohanji was standing in front of her along with Baba, and in the same blessing position which I used to see often in my dreams. After her PET scan, my mother told me about her experience and asked me if Mohanji wears kurta and dhoti. She gave me a description of his footwear also. I was amazed to hear that as she had never met Mohanji personally, yet gave me his full description. When Mohanji physically came to give her his darshan, she told him that he was wearing the same outfit as when he gave her darshan astrally. Mohanji told her that he was going to wear a T-shirt with jeans, but just to make her realise that he came to bless her, he wore that. He told her that she has a heart to heart connection with him. As her call for him was so strong, he had to come to her to fulfil her main desire. When she told him about Baba Sai and Mohanji coming together during her PET scan, Mohanji mentioned that a son can't be separated from his father. All Masters are one and it was proved to me when so many divine souls, Baba Sai, Mohanji and Mohanji's family came to visit mother.

Mohanji actually took very good care of my mother and she didn't even get to know that she had fourth stage cancer. It was a continuous prayer to Baba Sai and Mohanji and due to that, she was full of life till her last breath. To have a living Guru in our lives is the biggest asset and without letting us know even a bit, he does so much for us. And I started feeling him more in my mother as she had become complete love. I was seeing Divine Mother in her and more of Mohanji in her. In such a state, she was blessing and giving love to everyone, and Mohanji's family was witness to it, as they often used to come to meet her. When my mother started getting blood in her stools, it became a cause of worry, as she was feeling very weak. The doctor told us that she had a life expectancy of 6 to 12 weeks. But the most surprising thing was that she didn't have any kind of pain. The people who used to visit her were surprised as she was always smiling, full of love and life without any pains.

When I saw her in this state, suddenly Mohanji's voice started echoing in my ears. **"I'm doing what I can."**

One day I was shocked when I received a personal message from Neelu that Mohanji had taken on my mother's pain. It was shared in the global group by Preeti Duggal. But during that time, I was not checking my WhatsApp messages due to my busy schedule. As soon as I read about Mohanji's condition, I was in tears as he was having problems in his lungs the same as my mother. I couldn't control myself and called up Preeti to know about Mohanji's condition. The first thing she told me was about the blood in the stools, and I was speechless. My mother had blood in her stools three times, and the same thing had happened with Mohanji too. I couldn't stop crying. I hadn't said anything to Mohanji and just by connecting to his consciousness; he got to know and took everything on himself.

There is a big misconception that whosoever gets a chance to be with Mohanji physically is very fortunate. Indeed, they are very fortunate. But Mohanji works more in consciousness. He often reminds us to connect to his consciousness, guiding us to go within and become independent in every aspect.

Mohanji always stresses on doing our dharma properly. And I'm grateful to him that he gave me enough strength to serve my mother until 20th May. Mohanji was supposed to come that morning to meet my mother. And on the same day at 9 am, my Father fell in the market and my husband immediately took him to the doctor to get an X-ray done.

As Mohanji knows everything, he arrived at my place at 11:30 to meet my mother. She did his aarati and sang bhajans for him. And they had such a beautiful conversation related to Lord Krishna and Radha. Mohanji told her that death is not ugly, it's beautiful. He made her laugh and consoled her as she was really worried about my father, who was with the doctor for his X-ray. He gave us so much strength. There were so many things going on, but with his presence, we were feeling extremely light and were in a thoughtless state. My mother was in an ultimate state of bliss as her last desire of meeting Mohanji was fulfilled.

My father was also fortunate to meet Mohanji. Mohanji blessed him and told him in advance that it was a thigh bone fracture. My father was admitted on the same day for surgery. The same evening, my mother's health started deteriorating and she was admitted in ICU for breathlessness. My father also had surgery on the same day. I told Mohanji about my mother's condition, which he already knew. He said he's aware of my mother's condition. This is why he came and met her as a priority and told me not to worry as he's with her. It was a very tough situation for us. Mohanji told me that he's with both of them and he's reducing the intensity as much as possible. If not for Mohanji's grace, I would have collapsed in such a situation where I was feeling exhausted in every way.

In ICU, my mother was pouring unconditional love and blessings on everyone around her. My friends were meeting her daily as they wanted to take blessings from her. They felt Mohanji's immense energies in her. Her wish to meet Dr Wasir also got fulfilled when he came to meet her in ICU. During her last breath, she got a chance to listen to Mohanji Gayatri on the phone in Preeti's blissful voice. That was the last thing she heard. Mohanji didn't leave even a single desire of hers unfulfilled. When mother left her body, I was at peace as I knew that my Baba

Sai and Mohanji were standing beside her. Mohanji told me that I only concentrate on the rituals and to not forget to feed the sick, children, old women, animals and birds in her name. He's taking care of the rest and she's fine. So I need not worry.

On the 13th day after her death, which is the time for the soul's transition, my sister organised Mohanji's satsang at my place. When the playing list was on, Mohanji's Nirvana Shatakam also started playing automatically side by side. As before, through this obvious episode, I first strongly felt Mohanji's presence. We were surprised as Nirvana Shatakam is one of the rare verses written by Sri Adi Sankara Bhagavatpada, identifying himself as Lord Shiva and clearly explaining his theory of non-dualism. I was at peace to know that my mother was with Mohanji forever through this amazing experience. By chanting his name in her last days, my mother's soul merged into Guru's consciousness forever. The Guru does become the linking factor, a channel for putting the wandering lost soul back into contact with its source.

Mohanji, you were the light for me in the dark. You were always an inspiration and an aspiration. You made me come out of my ignorance. I learned to deal with my troubles, all due to you. Please keep me at your lotus feet always. I am nothing but the dust of your feet, my Gurudev.

SAVING GRACE

Lai Siong Chai, UK

In 2016, I was lucky to go to Kailash with Mohanji again. I was one of the 18 inner kora pilgrims. To be eligible to do the inner kora, one should have completed 12 rounds (circumambulations) of the Kailash outer kora pilgrimage. My pilgrimage of Kailash outer kora happened in 2014, the auspicious year of Dev Kumbh in which one round of Kailash is equal to 12 rounds. That granted me the eligibility for the inner kora.

Every step we took was not easy because of the high altitude and low oxygen levels. The path was also a loose rocky track with a frozen icy surface.

An incident happened on the second day of the parikrama, while we were crossing a stream with icy-cold, running water. Other pilgrims in the group jumped over easily to the opposite side of the stream. Without any doubt, I too just followed and jumped. Unfortunately, my pair of short legs didn't reach the opposite side fully, and I slid over. I fell on the ground, my right knee knocked on a stone causing pain. Instinctively I used my palms to support and prevent myself from falling further, not realising that the ground had a natural, sharp, black, stone flakes. I fell and heard my left palm slice open with a painful sound. I tried to withdraw my arm but somehow strained my right wrist instead. My head hit a rock and I blacked out. I was not sure how long I blacked out, but a Sherpa came and pulled me up from the ground. I soon got up, looked at my palm, rotated my wrist and checked my knee, and amazingly nothing seemed to have happened. I was wondering maybe because I had blacked out, I'd imagined being injured earlier. Without delay, I prepared to walk to catch up with the group. I lifted my head up and I saw that the sky had changed its colour from blue to entirely white, black and grey, indicating it was going to rain soon.

The 5 hour walk turned into a 13 hour walk, most of it in freezing rain. Finally, we reached the guest house. We walked into Mohanji's room; Devi was sitting on the edge of the bed waiting for our return. She let out a cry and told us that Mohanji was very ill. I kneeled down next to Mohanji and held his right hand; he twitched his hand and said his wrist was paining. I looked at his hand and saw that his wrist was swollen, and his left palm had two cuts and was bleeding. I stared at his bloodied hand, unable to think or move. Mohanji's palm was cut exactly at the place where I had cut my palm. His wrist and knee were also swollen. I burst into tears. I had witnessed how Mohanji protected and saved my life. This was beyond being a miracle. It is only a miracle to us because our human mind is not able to comprehend what had truly happened.

Cure from acute eczema

I had registered to join the retreat with Mohanji in the UK, in 2018. However, due to some family issues, I was unable to attend the same; hence I came to London to meet Mohanji before the programme.

The next day, I was invited to have lunch together

with Mohanji. Suddenly, we noticed that Mohanji had started to develop rashes on his arms. Everyone was worried and we were trying to find out what could have caused this allergy - food, washing powder or something else? Nothing could be concluded. We tried to apply some cream and even fresh Aloe Vera gel on Mohanji's arms, but nothing worked and his rashes were increasing. There was an open satsang that evening. When we returned from the satsang, we noticed that the rashes had spread to his legs too. Clearly, Mohanji was in great discomfort, but he didn't seem bothered at all. Everyone else was extremely worried except Mohanji.

While applying some Aloe Vera gel on Mohanji's legs, I noticed the shape of the rashes and was shocked. They seemed so familiar! I have had chronic rashes like eczema for many years. Even after using all sorts of creams and medications, nothing could cure it. I had suffered from this condition and had many sleepless nights. The itching was acutely uncomfortable. No remedy was of any help. I had just accepted this itching as a part of my life.

No one around me knew about my condition. However, after seeing Mohanji's rashes, I was reminded of my acute problem. I felt as if Mohanji had taken away my problem. This thought brought tears to my eyes. The next morning, I came to the house to say goodbye to Mohanji. I kneeled down in front of him and asked him why he had taken this from me? I had become used to it and I could bear it. He replied with a smile, **"All that had to go through my body. Only then will it be totally released and dissolved."** Mohanji's confirmation brought tears to my eyes again. Tears of gratitude. I was speechless. The tears kept flowing until I reached home which was a few hours away. I have no words to explain this grace and unconditional love from Mohanji.

Almost one and a half years since then, my itching and rashes have not returned! Truly, Mohanji released everything from me from the root! My years of suffering were dissolved in just a couple of days by taking it on to his own body, relieving me from enormous pain.

How can I describe this? Only love. Only grace. My gratitude will never be enough. I can only bow down at his lotus feet, my guru Mohanji!

MAGICAL HEALING IN MACHU PICCHU

Livia, Netherlands

This is a personal story. Being an introvert, I wasn't planning to write about it for a broad public, but I feel there is a reason for sharing which is beyond our preferences. May it reach those who were meant to read it.

For about ten years, I have been suffering from a lung condition, which is so rare that the medical profession doesn't have any expertise on it and therefore there is no appropriate treatment. My lung would collapse all of a sudden. In the beginning, it was every three to four months, later on, once per month or even more often. On most of the occasions, the collapse was partial, followed by a sharp pain in the upper chest area and shortness of breath. The pain would subside after some time, but the shortness of breath would last for days; and depending on the severity of the episode, sometimes for weeks.

The years 2014-2018 were really hard for me. I was physically quite weak but was doing my best to keep up with my daily schedule and house chores. Many people from my surroundings, who are not very close to me, hadn't noticed much, but I was exhausted all the time. When I finish my obligations, I would withdraw to recharge because my energy was very low. Also since 2014, I wasn't able to travel by plane because of this condition. The pressure change in the cabin during a flight could worsen my health. Living in Western Europe with parents and family in the Balkan region, it was quite a challenge to travel. Needless to say, it was exhausting me on different levels, the physical, but also the anticipation and fears connected to it ("what if it happens…," "will this ever come to an end," "would I be able to heal," and "what if it gets even more severe?").

Being a holistic therapist myself, I tried many modalities and nothing really gave tangible results.

When I met Mohanji in 2017 in Hvar (Croatia), where I travelled for three long days by train, bus and ferry and probably from the exhausting journey, by the end of it, I got another episode of a collapsed lung. I was weak and worried. Mohanji told me that the condition was to do with one of my previous lives and advised me to have a Mai-Tri session with Devi. During the session, Devi saw me in a war-like scene, being physically abused by men in uniform and an iron claw-kind of a weapon being forced into my chest. She didn't know anything about my problem at that point in time. The resemblance of this picture with the sharp pain in my chest I was feeling at the beginning of every episode was stunning.

My second retreat with Mohanji was at the Bosnian Pyramids in 2018. I came by airplane! It was my first flight after four years. I was already feeling Mohanji's protection and although my health was still not good with many collapses, pain, and weakness, I felt it'll be ok to fly. And it was.

Every time I met Mohanji, receiving his blessings,

cleansing, and with my practices and connection to his energy, my condition started improving gradually. I also started sessions with a healer who told me that my problem was of a karmic nature and therefore the modalities that are not addressing that deep level cannot have much impact. The collapses were gradually getting less frequent with more time to recuperate in between.

At the end of 2018, I saw the announcement of the Peru trip with Mohanji scheduled for April 2019. My first thoughts were: how great this journey must be, such beautiful nature, how magnificent it all looked in the photos and how precious the experiences were of the participants who went there the year before. The energy of the female principle, Shakti, the nurturing, soothing, beautiful energy of Pacha mama and the impact that it had on the people was heart-warming. But my rational mind reminded me of my condition, the flight of 14 hours and the altitude of the places where the pilgrimage was taking place. Yes, it looked great, but it wasn't for me. I dismissed the whole idea, maybe some other time. I just whispered to myself: if I have to go, I will get a sign, but I had no expectations as it really looked impossible.

One morning at the beginning of March just before waking up, I had such a clear dream of Mohanji. He was sitting at a big table together with many other people and I was sitting next to him. I had one question on my mind, regarding that trip to Peru, but I wasn't able to utter the question, although I wanted to ask. So he reached out to me, by telepathically asking me what the problem was with that trip…"Is it about the money?" "No," I answered, "It is about my condition…" then he said, "It'll be taken care of." I further said something like, "I was expecting a sign." He said, "Well, if this is not good enough…" I woke up in amazement, in complete awe! "This is extraordinary! I have never had a dream so clear before! I told my husband, and he acknowledged my thoughts and supported my intention to go. The same morning I wrote to the organization of the trip to ask if it was still possible to apply since it was only one month to the beginning of the program. And of course, it was!

This was quite a long introduction, but necessary to explain how this Peru trip happened for me in the first place. The preparations for the trip were made in a very short time. I would lie if I said that I wasn't anxious or that my mind didn't doubt the whole 'invitation' dream. But I was committed to go and really happy that I was going, despite all odds. Just before the trip, I googled a couple of names of the other participants and amongst them all, I remembered a lady, Thea, a Mai-Tri practitioner from the US who looked very light and seemed to have fine energy. I thought to myself how nice it would be if I could have a chance to talk to that lady… and sure enough a couple of days later, although the original schedule was different, Thea was sitting in the same mini-bus (transfer to the hotel) at the airport in Cusco together with one other lady from the US! So, the three of us travelled together, had a beautiful exchange of life stories and great fun. What a perfect beginning to the journey! I already felt that soothing, feminine energy that I was so looking forward to.

Over the next few days, when we were travelling from the hotel to the places of interest, I was again sitting next to Thea on the bus. As she already knew about my health concerns, she offered to do a Mai-Tri session for me, right there on the bus! I was really pleased with her offer and thankfully accepted it. She did a couple of sessions on different bus trips. She would invoke Mohanji's presence and his energy was palpable to her. It was very special and a little surreal because Mohanji in his physical body was sitting in the front line of the same bus!!

Although I feel weak and exhausted at home, I felt very energetic during the whole Peru pilgrimage. I felt a lot of soothing energies, lots of love from the group members and people surrounding us. I climbed to the Sun Gate of Machu Picchu, walked and chatted with people, in some places at the altitude of almost 4000m without any physical issues! It was completely unbelievable from the perspective of a rational mind!

On the last day on a bus to an Inka site, I sat next to Mohanji. That was my first chance on this trip to talk to Mohanji about my personal issues. We talked about ways of protection from negative energies, expressing positivity, non-doership and some personal issues that I brought up. He gave me some practical advice and then said, "You are much more liberated now than when you came here!" I looked at him a bit puzzled. He said, "Your lung, how is it now?" Then it occurred to me that I was breathing with full lung capacity with no pain! I really felt liberated at being able to freely move, walk, and climb mountain trails without any pain, shortage of breath or tiredness. How smoothly it was all going for me and how different it was compared to my state of health I was experiencing at home. Mohanji was tirelessly working on me and the result was really liberating! I was immensely happy, but I was also wondering if I was going to be able to keep this state and stay liberated from the pain and suffering after I return home and resume my 'normal life.'

Now we are almost eight months later in linear time and I still feel and cherish the gift I've got from Mohanji on the Peru trip. I still feel quite well physically and much more at peace mentally. Although I am a worrying type of person, I haven't been anxious or thinking much of the possibility that the condition might reoccur. I am much more at peace with my health. The condition is still not completely gone, but the episodes occur less frequently and they are far milder than they used to be. I have started travelling by plane again on a regular basis!

I feel deep gratitude to Mohanji for healing me on many levels. I feel that the healing started as soon as I connected with him for the first time and culminated during the Peru trip last spring. But of course, the journey doesn't end there. I'm still 'rowing my boat' and the weather changes. After this experience of healing that is so real and unquestionable to me, and after practically experiencing what Mohanji meant by "It'll be taken care of," deep in my being, I now feel that I can relax and have faith.

Thank you Mohanji, for this wonderful experience!

Grace that Heals

Thank you for your work and availability to every being that asks or connects to you in any way! Thank you for your teachings, they make my journey smoother and my life much more meaningful!

Guru Leela

Grace that Heals

BIRTH OF TRUE SELF

Milica Bulatovic, South Africa

> *We are one consciousness. I am never away from you. There is no existence in separation. Beingness is unity. We are one and never separate. – Mohanji*

I would like to share the recent experience that led me to complete peace through faith in my Guru Brahmarishi Mohanji, and acceptance of life's circumstance that most people would call difficult or even extreme.

It all started with the birth of my second daughter, Sofia Sage, on 19th January, 2018. In Serbia, this day is called Bogojavljenje, meaning the day God appeared. My first realisation was that I couldn't label her as mine. I would look at other mothers in the room in the ICU and couldn't understand why we call children ours. She belonged to everyone equally as she belonged to me. She had incredible energy of peace and serenity in the first few days until the pain took over. She had very powerful energy too that I only realised after she left her physical body.

Doctors had diagnosed her with a rare congenital heart disease which was inoperable. Through the grace of Mohanji, I gathered the courage to accept this and live each day in full faith. The doctors could not understand my decision to continue with the pregnancy when they had informed me of this in the 5th month of pregnancy. They had advised immediate termination! In my heart, I could never even think of termination. How can it be my choice? From day one, we didn't receive any warmth or helpful assistance from the doctors and this carried on till the last day of Sofia's short life. But to live with integrity is the only way, no matter what others may say. They only see from their level of understanding.

I always believed that everything in life happens for a reason and so did the birth of this incredible soul that graced us with her presence for just a short time. I still gave it my all, did all the research as well as consulted the best specialists in the country to offer the best service to Sofia. After everyone confirmed the same prognosis, I settled into acceptance and looked after her the best I could do with the awareness that I had. There were many challenging moments and a week would seem like a year, but I flowed from one situation to the next without getting or experiencing thoughts of hardship. My mantra was to stay natural and be myself at all times no matter what others may say. If I needed to cry, I did. It would be just for a few minutes and I would feel lighter as I wouldn't lose myself in emotions. The understanding of what was really happening would come and I would learn more about myself in this way. I didn't realize that by choosing this mantra, I chose to fully accept myself which led me to more powerful experiences. My heart was opening and embracing all situations instead of closing down with fear. I learnt this is where true strength lies, in acceptance and love.

People were telling me that I was going through so

much, but I could immediately think of many other situations happening somewhere else that were much worse. I simply didn't feel any pain. I started to understand that when something triggers painful emotions this only means that we have those unresolved emotions from the past within us. Something that also made a huge difference was the understanding I had that Sofia's soul chose this experience and it was mainly for our growth and learning.

We spent many weeks in hospital and those were the most trying days. We had to share a room with many other people, and other children in pain crying sometimes for even 24 hours. Sofia was incredible. She allowed it all to happen even though every movement of her body was so uncomfortable. She would cry a lot but she still chose to stay with us. I remember every time we had one or two good days, a glimpse of hope would come to me that she is doing better. She would get worse very soon to keep me from getting off the road of acceptance and telling me that she is not staying.

Whenever I was at a breaking point physically, help arrived and we just carried on until one day a palliative care doctor came and told me that we could take Sofia home even if she was on oxygen, fed through the nasogastric tube and on morphine. At first, I was really surprised because it had never occurred to me and she warned me that Sofia may also leave us at any moment and we had to be prepared for that. At first, that really scared my husband and me, but I wanted us to go home and be in a peaceful environment as it was becoming unbearable in the hospital. I went with the flow of events and I felt that was exactly what we needed. Guidance would come from Mohanji's quotes, blogs and even telepathically. This is how I stayed in peace most of the time. Just observed everything and higher awareness would just come, guide me and teach me. When we are based firmly in truth, nothing can unbalance us. Looking back, it is very obvious now how every event in life happens for a reason. We can choose to be emotional about it or accept and learn from it. When we learn from it, we honour life. We realise that life is a gift when used for a higher purpose. Then no pain will ever affect you. This is what Sofia showed us. We are given life, but we don't own it. This body is on lease from God, choose wisely and consciously what to do with it. Life is truly a gift.

I just observed everything completely neutrally, no reference points, watching and responding to all of Sofia's needs and the other drama that was happening with people around me. At a certain point, I had to have the help of a nurse at home as feeding became challenging and there was so much more. Simply, one person couldn't look after her any more. To find the right person took a long time. As I would finish training one nurse, something would happen and they would leave for many different reasons. It was becoming very tiring and didn't feel like we received help at all.

Until one day, in the last week of Sofia's life, an incredible person came into our lives. Gladys was just perfect. Gladys knew when to leave us alone for privacy and when to take over. She would know when to speak and when to be silent. So non-intrusive unlike most were. She learned fast all that needed to be done and I felt like she was an extension of me. As in many such moments, I realized how we should never really worry even for a second. Again, the flow of life brought the right person when it was necessary and when certain karma was resolved.

When we express our true nature to the world, there are no roles to play. I didn't identify with the role of a mother to Sofia. I didn't get lost in that identification. I was just neutral, giving her all the love possible and not getting caught in emotions. To be honest at certain still moments while I was holding her, it felt like she knew everything. She was aware of so much more. In those quiet moments, it felt like an exchange of energy and awareness. When she looked at you she looked through you. I always sensed she can see it all. Her look was like looking at eternity. No beginning, no end.

Two days before she left her body, I was gifted a very special afternoon. It was a public holiday and it was very peaceful at home. A very pleasant and sunny day. Sofia needed me to hold her that day. She was becoming very uncomfortable so I held her in my arms while she was sleeping and we sat in the garden the whole afternoon. The energy was incredible. I felt pure grace surround us. As my elder daughter Sara joined us, she felt it instantly too. It felt like hundreds of angels were sitting with us. Sara shared that there was the presence of the Masters. I felt truly grateful for that day and it still feels like a dream. It was interesting that my sister dreamt that night that we were all sitting at my home surrounded by Masters! The next morning, she shared her dream with me.

That night Sofia got very unwell and the next day was hardest for all. She clearly was in huge discomfort and could barely breathe. It seemed like, the previous day gave me all that I needed to be completely calm and give her all my pure love and care. For some people who were with us that day, it was unbearable. But when I allowed myself to flow, an invisible force, Mohanji's grace took over. I realised that once you let go of concepts, you simply flow. If the mind is still, there is no reference point, every moment is like new. No heaviness stays with you.

So I didn't recognize the situation as hard or difficult and I could respond better to her needs. Mohanji had explained to me that she was an elevated soul and that this happens very rarely that such a soul comes as a blood relation. I felt blessed. She decides when she will go and she knows what is best. The last day came and I was alone with Sofia as she was in a coma since the night before, so there was no need for any help. I did all my chanting, performed Sai Baba aarati (which started playing on its own) and Mohanji aarati and sat in complete peace with her.

It was on the 29th of April. She left at the exact moment the moon was ascending on Buddha Poornima – the day when Ganeshananda Giri left his body two years ago. This was also Avadhoota Nadananda's birthday. What an auspicious day!

She attained the highest and chose the exact time for 'rocket speed dissolution' as Mohanji wrote to me. At the moment of her passing, Sofia and I merged forever in love without a trace of pain or sadness. When we love unconditionally, there is no room for pain or any emotion. That morning, there was a magnificent pink sunrise. Pink was never my colour of choice but lately, I often see it. Even the sunset was pink for a few days after. So I checked the meaning of this colour and found out that pink is the colour of the universal love of oneness!

Every moment is important as it is given to us to fulfill our purpose. Our breath is given to us. Two years ago, when I was attending a weekend program with Mohanji, he had asked all the participants to share what they had learned during the programme. I shared that there is nothing to do, but just be.

Today I feel that there is no need to even be. Just merge.

There is nothing to express but You.

I find my home in You.

This came to me as, even the need to contemplate, stopped.

As Sofia took her last breath, I felt her become part of me or I became part of her. It was not a heavy moment. It was a moment of freedom. Her body was finally pain-free, and I understood that she never suffered as she was fulfilling her purpose. When the purpose is clear, nothing can stand in your way.

Numerous miracles were experienced after her passing. I felt completion and subtlety that I didn't feel before. Mohanji gave me the strength to face it all, and held me tight and cleared the way and did so much more than we could ever know.

The ability to love and expand our hearts is where we find our true nature. Our true rebirth is in our hearts. I was given Sofia by Mohanji and the Tradition, what was best for the completion of karma and my spiritual growth. It was all perfectly orchestrated for higher elevation and higher awareness of miracles of life. For a long time now, I have had a feeling of amnesia, that there is so much to remember and nothing to learn. Now it feels that it is the remembrance of my true being that has begun.

None of the experiences and inner discoveries would have been possible without Mohanji. From the depth of my being, I wish love and light to all. May we all wake up to the truth with his guidance and love. With surrender and deep gratitude to Mohanji.

Guru Leela

Grace that Heals

A DATE WITH DESTINY
Natesh Ramsell, USA

By finding out about Mohanji and having the opportunity to meet him halfway around the world just a few weeks later, in March 2016 was filled with wonderful synchronicity! And how quickly it developed into a deep and powerful connection continues to amaze me! The latter is due in large part to the fact that I have been connected to the traditions of India since 1975, and connected strongly with my first Guru in 1979, despite my heavy skepticism about the whole notion of a Guru and the major hurdle of having a Western-educated analytical mind. Through sheer and abundant grace, I was given experiences that enabled me to get past those hurdles and my life changed dramatically for the better. While there is much to that story and the many experiences I have been blessed to have with Mohanji in the few short years since meeting him, my focus here is on coming to know of and meeting Mohanji, and a few instances that display what appear to be clear capacities beyond the normal state that give us a glimpse of Mohanji's stature.

In early 2016, I decided it was finally time to take my first trip to India. It certainly took me a long time for several different reasons, and many of my friends were quite surprised to learn it would be my first visit. Although I had decided to join a planned pilgrimage with some other Americans, I also was inspired to visit the mahasamadhi shrine of my first Guru and in preparation for the trip, did an internet search on how to visit his samadhi shrine. As the Universe would have it, I first clicked on a link near the top of the search results that took me to a blog on the 'mohansuniverse' Wordpress site. Reading the blog I found there is when I first heard of Mohanji. I immediately wondered who Mohanji is and why had he visited that samadhi shrine?" I clicked a link on the blog site to 'mohanji.org' and began soaking it all up – starting with information about who Mohanji is and his transformation, discovering that he gives shaktipat (a profound transfer of spiritual energy from Master to disciple that I first experienced with my first Guru) and then watching a few videos and discovering he gives satsangs in English. I was immediately drawn in by his clarity, warmth and keen focus on liberation and wondered if there was any way I might be able to meet him during my trip to India.

Happily, I learned that there was a weekend program 'near Mumbai' that of course lined up perfectly with the end of the pilgrimage already booked. Given that the program would be in India, I figured it might not be in English nor with translation to English, but that didn't matter as I just wanted to experience meeting Mohanji and being around him for a couple of days.

My entire first visit to India was extraordinary, and in retrospect, I can't think of a better way for it to have concluded than meeting Mohanji and attending that weekend program with him. He gave a satsang in English and was very personable, accessible and approachable – the latter two qualities in particular certainly being a new and welcoming experience for me! As with other powerful Masters, the spiritual energy when being with Mohanji shifts my consciousness into subtly altered states.

I also had the profound blessing to be asked by him to chant while he was giving shaktipat on the final day. I asked that my shaktipat be at the end, so I could be sure to be 'functional' for chanting. When it was my turn, I came in front of Mohanji and knelt down. He put his thumb on my third eye and rested his fingers on my crown, as with the others. The energy was powerful and my body gently convulsed several times in reaction to the kundalini shakti coursing through it. Just as he removed his hand from my head, I glanced up at him and his face was completely still and expressionless and his eyes in Shambhavi mudra, gazing upwards with eyelids half-closed, and I could only see the 'whites' of his eyes. It was as if the man Mohanji I had experienced as warm, welcoming, funny and approachable wasn't even there! After that, I sat quietly for a while to let the energy 'sink in'.

I went on a blissful 'Mohanji binge' after that first weekend! Three weeks later, I attended a weekend program with him in Virginia, and then wound up unexpectedly also going to spend time with him in Canada, directly from Virginia. About a month later, in May 2016, I attended the Bosnian Pyramids retreat, which was truly remarkable.

In June 2016, about a month after returning from the Bosnia trip, I drove to Southern California to lead the kirtan at a weekend conference. It was at a resort which had several hot-spring pools at different temperatures that we would enjoy in the evenings. On the last night there, I decided to take a final dip in the hot springs, but as I was headed through the lobby to get to the pools, I started strangely feeling a little dizzy. But when I got out of the hot spring pool a little later, I felt fine. The next day, I drove to the coast to spend a couple of days and I had another episode. A third one happened the next day while visiting a Hindu temple in Malibu. All three times, it only lasted 20-30 minutes and then I was fine. A couple of hours after the one at the temple, I started my roughly 500-mile solo drive home to Sedona, Arizona.

A few hours into my journey, I got a call from Ganesh, who heads Mohanji Foundation USA. He asked if I was feeling okay and told me that Mohanji had contacted him a couple of times to ask him if he had spoken with me. Ganesh said he got the impression Mohanji was concerned about me so he decided to call and check on me. As I was feeling fine at the time –not even recalling the 3 dizziness spells at that moment – I replied that I was fine and there was nothing to worry about, so I didn't know why Mohanji would be asking how I'm doing. However, I experienced yet another spell several hours later when I got out of my car in North Phoenix with about a 90-minute drive yet to go to my home in Sedona. It was about 11:30 pm and I was pretty tired, so I napped in the car until about 1 am and resumed the trip home, arriving at about 2:30 am.

The next morning, I was feeling a bit dizzy again and when I started to say something to Monnie (my wife), the words came out garbled – I could not properly form or pronounce the words I was meaning to say! While she had been concerned that I might be having a stroke when I was still in California, now with the slurred speech it was obvious that was what was happening and we wasted no time in getting me to the ER right away. My pulse was dropping below 40, triggering an alarm and the initial thought was heart trouble. Though I could walk, they didn't even want me walking 30 feet to the restroom without being monitored and supervised. Later that night, I was taken to the hospital in a neighbouring town by ambulance so that I would continually be monitored. The short version of what happened there is that it was determined that I had indeed had a stroke, and the heart concern turned out to be unfounded after several tests, including an angiogram.

After a few days, I was transferred to a rehabilitation hospital in an even more distant town, which had been recommended because the stroke had been serious enough to warrant it. My recovery was remarkably swift and mostly complete. Unlike the rest of the patients at the rehab hospital, I could walk on my own, though I was chided the first night by the nurses for leaving my room unsupervised to take a walk in the corridors. My speech improved so quickly that by the time I had my first appointment with a speech therapist the next day, she said it wouldn't be necessary to have any further appointments because she really couldn't help me further. I just needed to keep talking!

The partial paralysis on the left side was not severe

but I was not able to play chords on the guitar with my left hand when I arrived. The next day, I could form the chords, although slowly and pretty much one finger at a time, and the day after, I could change from chord to chord slowly. And the following day, I could much more easily and quickly change from one chord to another. As much as I've relied on playing the guitar to support my devotional chanting, this was huge for me! At my first session with the occupational therapist, she learned that I played the guitar and at the next session, I was giving her a guitar lesson! I had been scheduled to be there for 5 to 7 days and was out in less than 72 hours! The one thing that took longer to recover (and remains a bit of an issue) is my balance, for which I continued with outpatient therapy for several weeks after returning home.

I was calm and in a 'good frame of mind' throughout. When I could play the guitar doing chord changes still somewhat tentatively, I posted a video of my chanting from the rehab hospital. Many friends remarked about my positive attitude at the time. I do not doubt that Mohanji's grace and protection helped minimize the situation and speed up my recovery. Interestingly, one of the comments on that video post was: "Of course you are making surprising progress! You have powerful beings helping you!" Watching that video again recently reminded me of how the left side of my mouth was not even moving properly due to the partial paralysis to my left side.

Ganesh communicated with me during the first few days in the hospital and let me know that Mohanji was asking about me and that he wanted me to know that he was with me and protecting me. However, by the time I came home, I had forgotten all about that initial call from Ganesh during my drive back from California and the messaging back and forth over the next few days. It was a few months before I remembered that call and when I did, I was awed by the fact that Mohanji had tuned into what was going on with me from halfway around the world before I had even realized the seriousness!

Fast forward to August 2018, and I was attending a weekend program with Mohanji in Virginia. Several of us had travelled there from Sedona and we were blessed to have a short group meeting with Mohanji during one of the breaks. The topic of the nature of his expanded awareness came up and I shared how Mohanji had been aware of the fact that I was having this major health issue from halfway around the world before I was even aware. It was then that he commented that there had been 'intervention' from the beginning, so that the effects would be greatly reduced and that there would be more of a series of minor experiences instead of the major one that would have otherwise happened. I did indeed have that series of what seemed just short and minor dizzy spells that turned out to be warnings of something more major happening.

Though perhaps I 'should have' known, and quietly felt that I had been helped more than I knew, this direct confirmation from Mohanji was a powerful revelation and all I could do was express my deepest, humblest gratitude at that moment. It is truly a blessing to be both guided and protected by Mohanji and the entire Tradition of Liberation which he represents. I am forever grateful and offer my most humble prostrations to the Consciousness we know as Mohanji!

A GIFT OF A NEW LIFE!

Neelima Vepu, India

To describe a Master's grace upon us is a very difficult task, as we with our limited human faculties, cannot understand the extent to which a Master helps a devotee to cross the quagmire of Karma. Here is one such humble attempt of mine about how Mohanji saved my mother from a painful health issue.

In March 2019, my mother had developed some gynaecological problems, wherein she was advised to have a hysterectomy, after the usual rounds of tests, including a biopsy. Thankfully, the tests did not reveal anything to trigger panic, but the operation was mandatory to avoid any future problems that could occur considering her age.

Before this, my mother never faced any serious health issues, and this would be the first time she would be admitted to a hospital. The thought of seeing her on a hospital bed was making me feel extremely depressed. But I reassured myself that Mohanji was taking care of everything. We planned to have her operation in May, as it would be summer vacation for my kids and I could be with my parents to help them through this period.

On the morning of the operation, while my mother was under the knife, I went on a chanting mode (Mohanji Gayatri Mantra) all through that duration. The operation was successful! However, the ordeal started the next day. She was coughing constantly and the X-Ray reports showed a severe lung infection in spite of all the antibiotics that had been injected, as is always done after surgery. Her coughing continued for two days continuously.

She couldn't take anything orally even after three days of operation. Her haemoglobin level had dropped considerably. She had become so weak that she was unable to speak even for a minute. Adding to her troubles, she developed dysentery. The oxygen levels in her blood went so low that, she had to be put on an oxygen mask.

Unable to find the cause of the lung infection in this hospital, the doctors advised her to be shifted to another hospital, to get more tests done, to know the cause of the lung infection. While my mother was going through all these, I messaged Mohanji to take care of her and relieve her from the suffering. He replied that he was taking care of her. He also said that one has to go through these things and changing their course would affect them negatively. He advised me to do a few things to reduce her karma, which I did immediately. I was very frightened, seeing her in this situation, but I had the faith that Mohanji was working on her. A few days later, she was shifted to yet another big hospital, and all the necessary tests and scans were done to find out the cause of the lung infection. By his grace, all the tests were normal, but she was still on oxygen.

She was also given distant Mai-Tri. As a Mai-Tri practitioner, I also gave her Mai-Tri. Interestingly, my mother would feel Mohanji's hand on her head, even after I would remove mine. She could feel his loving and gentle energy healing her. Slowly but gradually, her condition improved. She started taking solid food and all her complications gradually started decreasing. Mohanji's grace was visible.

The critical case, which was being referred to the ICU (Intensive Care Unit), was easily transformed into a positively responding case. Her dysentery stopped, the haemoglobin count became normal, the lung infection reduced considerably, the persistent cough was gone, and the oxygen saturation levels returned to normal. In a couple of days, she was able to breathe normally without any external support. After a week's stay in the new hospital, she was declared fit to be discharged.

A normal post-surgery five-day stay in the hospital got extended into a 12-day long stay! But all is well, and that ends well! Now she is recovering very fast, which is Mohanji's grace in full bloom.

Mohanji, not only took care of my mother, but he took care of me as well in this tough time. I was with my mother, the whole time with almost no sleep and no rest in the hot summer for 12 days. I had to shuttle between our house and the hospital in the hot sun, to take care of my kids and to cook. I could feel his energy take over, whenever I felt exhausted. He always consoled me whenever I would cry at my mother's painful condition. He gave me the mental and physical strength to go through all this. It was a real ordeal to see my mother lying so helplessly for days together and at the same time to put up a brave face in front of everyone and cheer up my mother. He made me take care of my mother as a small baby. It was Mohanji everywhere. I always felt, only he existed, I was nowhere present.

Any volume of words would fall short to express my gratitude to the unconditional love and protection Mohanji showers upon us. Thank you, my Gurudev for everything. Love you forever.

INNER TRUTH
NellyAnne Noronha, UK

Today, I feel especially grateful. Miracles do happen when you have faith! For a couple of months in 2018, I had a gynaecological condition where I was getting excessive bleeding. The doctors had done several scans and found no abnormalities apart from a very small fibroid which they said was negligible. Since they could not find any solutions, they said the only option I had was to have a hysterectomy. Now I'm smiling because something that was said to be impossible actually wasn't. I honestly respect doctors, modern medicine, their hard work, and dedication. On the other hand, something in me refused to accept that removing an organ is the only solution. I tried almost everything and many times I was disappointed, although I'm grateful to all the people who tried to help me. Sometimes, doctors' voices were very scary, but even then I knew that something else could be done. I knew that there was still something sitting inside of me that I had to let go.

I had been watching Mohanji's videos on YouTube and I watched a video where he explains the tremendous protection and healing that one receives by simply listening to the Shiva Kavacham. Since then, I was eager to receive it. I mentioned this to a friend who directed me to another video on YouTube on Shiva Kavacham which I listened to without missing a day before I went to bed, for 3 months. I then had an opportunity to attend a 'Shiv Mahapuran Katha' (story of Shiva), after which for some reason, I stopped listening to the YouTube Shiva Kavacham video.

In August 2018, I was finally blessed to attend Mohanji's satsang and meditation in London for the very first time. During the meditation, I constantly invoked Bhagawan Nityananda, a great saint whose samadhi shrine is in Ganeshpuri, India. I got home and was attracted to Mohanji's picture displaying his eyes on the internet. I woke up the following morning and again in my meditation I kept invoking Bhagawan Nityananda and Mohanji's picture kept coming up in front of me. It was Mohanji's sheer grace and blessings that I not only miraculously got the Shiva Kavacham chanted by Mohanji through one of Mohanji's followers from Australia, but also got connected to Subhasree in the UK.

Since then, I listened to the Shiva Kavacham recited by Mohanji, every single day. I believe this helped me to go deep within myself, to remove many blockages. I began reading Mohanji's blogs, and about his retreats, meditations, and healings (visible as well as the invisible healings). I realised all the techniques that he used were there only to guide us to ourselves. I started listening to my inner voice; you can call it intuition, and felt I was on the right path. Actually, I didn't have any doubts. I am eternally grateful.

I contacted Subhasree for a Mai-Tri session. However, as she was out of town then, she suggested in addition to listening to the Shiva Kavacham, to recite Mohanji's Gayatri 108 times every day and she would do Mai-Tri within a week, on her return.

She told me "Don't worry; things will be alright," as she had spoken to Mohanji and he had said, "Just do a single Mai-Tri session."

A week later, Subhasree did Mai-Tri for me. During the session, I realised that every disease, when it's already on a physical level, is only the manifestation of what has been sitting inside us for a long, long time - suppressed emotions. If you don't cure the root cause of the problem, the problem will appear again and again. I felt that as the only truth. And it was! Immediately, a week later, my month-long bleeding stopped. My intention here is not to tell you - go away from your doctors and don't take any prescribed medicines. But that is not the only answer. I was personally then directed to take ayurvedic medicine where I had to follow a strict vegan diet, which helped regulate the monthly gynaecological rhythm of the body.

Even if you don't have a Guru, my only advice which I also learnt from dearest Mohanji and experienced myself would be to listen to your body. Listen to yourself. Spend time with yourself. Get to know yourself. Something is sitting inside you; maybe anger, hatred, sorrow, pains from the past, or guilt. Find it, face it, and let it go. Don't run away from it, it won't go. How you feel is important. Emotional health is directly linked to physical health. Be positive but don't be 'artificially' positive. Keep emptying yourself from all the negative things that are sitting inside you and making you sick, although it takes time and effort. Love yourself and do not give up!

How can I ever repay what Mohanji has done for me? Since then, I have been blessed to participate in seva opportunities, miraculously visit Sai Baba in Shirdi, and Bhagawan Nityananda's samadhi in Ganeshpuri. I surrender everything with utmost humility and gratitude to Mohanji and the entire Tradition.

Guru Leela

Grace that Heals

FROM SELF-HATE TO SELF-ACCEPTANCE

Nikolina Dragojević, Serbia

It was my fifth year at the Bosnian Pyramids with Mohanji. Just like every other program with Mohanji (and being on this Path), a lot of acceptance and flexibility was required to pull off the logistics. 100+ participants, 10+ locations, unpredictable weather, and our flexibility was being tested.

One nice morning, I woke up with my throat completely closed. 'Closed' meaning I couldn't swallow anything: food, water, not even my saliva. I wasn't surprised as I have been struggling with my throat for many years already and this has happened before, 3 years ago, at the Bosnian Pyramids as well.

That year in 2016, I managed to get through the entire 5-day program only with the IV (intravenous) therapy – no food/water/supplements. My energy was high, my mood was great like nothing was happening, I managed to climb all the pyramids with no struggle. What would be the usual reaction to that? Impossible! But, 'impossible' does not exist in the dictionary of Mohanji's Path.

This 2019, the same thing happened in the middle of the programme. I just woke up one day and couldn't swallow. Not surprised at all, because I was aware of some internal battles happening that might cause this. I went for 2 days without food and water before we decided it was time to get IV therapy and ask Mohanji what to do.

I knew what the trigger was. A few days before the Bosnian Pyramids programme, I was in a situation where I felt like I didn't do any good, I failed, I wasn't good enough, I was misunderstood, and not accepted for who I was. All sorts of insecurities were coming to the surface. As advised by Mohanji, we called Zoran, an amazing man and a great kinesiologist from Sarajevo, who did the treatment and told me things that were lying deep inside me causing this reaction.

The following morning it was time to decide if I should continue travelling with Mohanji and go to Slovenia, as the team there needed support for the upcoming programme, or if I should go back home to Serbia. Going to Slovenia was risky as there was no one to give me IV and I didn't have insurance. Plus it's a very long journey of more than 8 hours and I hadn't eaten for 4 days, but I would travel with Mohanji.

When we asked him what to do, he insisted that it was up to me and how my body felt. **"You should not suffer; you should do what's natural to you."** Just the night before, Zoran and I had discussed how indecisive I was, and here I was in a position to make a big decision.

But Mohanji also gave me the biggest lecture and so much clarity as to why this was happening. The situation mentioned earlier was just a trigger. But the cause lay much deeper. My self-hate and lack of self-acceptance were causing this. I was punishing my body and denying food and water to my body, not taking care of myself. Self-criticizing, self-judging, self-hating. On the opposite side is self-acceptance.

Mohanji will not interfere with my karmic constitution, but he is giving me a platform which I can use to change that. Now! I have to stop criticising, comparing, judging myself, and others. We all have our strengths and weaknesses. I just need to make one conscious decision. Self-acceptance! When we accept ourselves, life becomes purposeful. We become purposeful and powerful.

My eyes were full of tears. Every single word was hitting hard and straight in the centre. He is giving a platform, he is giving energy, and he is empowering us. But we need to take that one step. How often do you meet someone who is straight to the point, so honest, open and direct? And gives you just what you need at that point. Probably more than what we are even aware of and can understand. Will we ever be able to understand?

I had a big urge to go to Slovenia, but now I wasn't sure if I was being masochistic (and choosing to suffer) or I really should go. With a little push by lovely friends, I decided to have more faith, surrender, and go to Slovenia. With a hidden smile on his face, when Mohanji said, "Very good" I knew; whatever happened, it was going to be okay.

Devi was sitting in the car seat next to me, just in case I needed a Mai-Tri session on the way. Somewhere halfway, I started feeling nausea and weakness.

Devi started with Mai-Tri and I was feeling worse by the second. Nausea was getting stronger and stronger.

I used to constantly wonder how I would vomit with this tight throat and oesophagus, was it even possible, would I choke... And here I was, in the car, on the way to Slovenia, with a completely closed throat and a strong urge to vomit. With so much pain and not being able to breathe properly, thoughts of panic started coming up. At that moment, I was just telling myself, "But he is sitting in front of you, what could happen to you?" I was getting calmer, started vomiting and all of a sudden, the pain was gone. We took a quick break at the petrol station and there was me wondering if I could vomit which also meant that I could swallow as well, right? And yes, I could. My throat opened up and I could have a cup of tea after 4 days of being without food and water. What a blessing!

It's not just that he is there holding our hand all the way, helping us, guiding us, but he is there to empower us to deal with all our insecurities and fears. I know there is still a long way for me to go. I could feel a lot of blockages still in my body, in my throat. I could swallow but not nearly as well as before the trip to Bosnia. I went back home and started contemplating on everything he had told me in Bosnia. "Self-acceptance. More positivity. No judging. No criticizing. No comparing. Take care of yourself so that you can give unconditionally to others."

All my non-acceptance and self-hate peaked the

moment I was told I won't be able to go to Kailash. Every single negative thought that was there come to the surface. Every single one. 'I'm not worth it, I'm not good enough. I'm not doing enough. I don't even belong to this Path. Why am I here? What for? Do I need all of this in my life? What's the purpose?' I started comparing myself to others. I started feeling resentment towards some close people from the team. Why was I even given the hope that there was a chance for me to go?

I had a meeting that I needed to attend at that time and I was on edge, not wanting to pick up the call. Why? Why would I do this? I can't do it anymore. I don't want it. Tears were running down my face as never before. Negative thoughts were suffocating me. I cried uncontrollably and was overwhelmed by sadness. I could never have imagined I would react in this way. I couldn't believe what was happening.

But one thing in me was strong – awareness. I could feel and differentiate the negative thoughts that were mine and the negative thoughts that were coming from outside. I had the awareness that all the comparisons and resentment wasn't mine. And I was able to discard it. I was aware that this shall pass as well. I had the awareness that there was a bigger picture to all this. I had the awareness that this was a big cleansing; a big test for me. I managed to get up, take the call, and complete the meeting as though nothing had happened. Then I went back to bed to cry.

The next day I woke up feeling a little sad, but much better. I had a Mai-Tri session with Milica. There was so much clarity. I felt so much positivity. I felt so much lighter. Like something big had fallen off my shoulders. I knew what I had to do. Just to have faith and keep moving, keep walking, accepting myself.

That night I woke up with the feeling that I had something in my mouth. I thought it was the homoeopathic medicine that I had taken before going to bed. But when I took it out, it was a stapler pin! Metal stapler pin! I was shocked. I remember very well brushing my teeth before bed, drinking water, taking homoeopathic medicine. There was no way this could appear in my mouth from some food.

My first thought was, "Oh my God what would have happened if this went through my throat?" I started feeling grateful to Mohanji for always taking care of me and being there for me. The following day when Milica spoke, I was told that it was a huge cleansing, some heavy energies were released and that was why the pin had appeared in my mouth.

Along with that big sign, that huge blockages were being removed, there were little signs as well that showed me I was trying, I was doing something for myself, I was taking that one step forward. I started drinking more water, and everyone who knows me knows that I would never drink, even 1l of water in 2-3 days. I stopped eating sugar, and everyone knows I'm the biggest sugar addict. I just adore chocolate!

And the biggest shock of all, I signed up for yoga

classes. In February 2019 during HSTY Teacher Training, the team was unable to convince me to do even 5 minutes of yoga in 10 days. And here I was starting yoga classes.

It was always clear to me that being with Mohanji means fire. It's always challenging, pushing the mind's boundaries. But despite the tough times, I remain here because I know why I'm here. He gives strength, he gives awareness. He empowers us to go through ups and downs, to (re-) discover the higher Self. He provides the possibilities and platforms for us to progress in life, to serve, to clear our garbage, to develop what we need and drop off what we don't need, and to grow.

He gives us everything we need, at a given moment, as per our capacity, without us asking for anything, even though we might not understand at that point. Sometimes it might not be easy, especially when tough situations happen. But I remain here, despite all the challenges. It is up to us to use this opportunity in the best possible way.

MIRACLES OF GRACE

Nirupma Chowdhary, India

Mohanji's presence in my life is indescribable! Each time I meet him, he says, **"Keep doing your work. I am with you."** His words motivate me to keep going.

I work at the Mohanji School of Supplementary Education for underprivileged children in Jammu. My seva for the children in this school not only brings me a lot of joy and satisfaction, but I also receive the unimaginable love and protection from Mohanji, not just for me but also for my family. While I serve these children, Mohanji is constantly looking after me and my family, physically and emotionally, at all levels. Not just once, but every time.

I will first share about the miraculous recovery of my daughter Sukriti from her 12 year-long chronic illness, with Mohanji's grace.

It was Feb 2016. Mohanji had come to Jammu and he visited our school. The essence of his advice that day to us was, to prepare yourselves and the children for any kind of calamity. Before he was about to leave, he asked me if I had the 'Shiva Kavacham' mantra chanted by him, with me. This mantra is a very sacred mantra chanted by Mohanji and considered very powerful. However, it is not just given to anyone. Mohanji himself asking me to have it was a great blessing and opportunity for me to get it. Little did I know at that point, Mohanji was protecting me with this mantra. Anyway, I was very happy to receive it and I listened to it as soon as I got home.

The next day, I heard some very distressing news. My daughter Sukriti who lives with her husband and 10 month-old daughter in London, was admitted to hospital due to severe diarrhoea and fever. She was extremely sick. As days passed with no improvement what so ever in her condition, we were getting extremely worried. Sukriti was unable to eat any food, was unable to retain anything in her stomach. Diarrhoea and fever continued. Doctors said if this situation continued for 14 days, then it may bring about a serious, lifelong issue, or even be life-threatening for her. With a 10 month-old baby, Sukriti's health condition was causing us all immense stress.

I finally managed to reach London on the 11th day. As she saw me, she burst out crying, "I want to live for my daughter." As a mother, to see my daughter in that frail condition and seeing her baby suffering, I was heartbroken. But I kept my faith in Mohanji. I felt very strong with the most powerful weapon from Mohanji that I had with me at that time. That was the Shiva Kavacham. I played Shiva Kavacham twice a day and Sukriti listened to it with all sincerity. The very next day, on the 12th day, Sukriti woke up with a much-improved condition. She even managed to eat mashed potato and her stomach retained it. Right on time, just two days before that 14th-day threat, Sukriti started her journey on the path of recovery. In the meantime, doctors diagnosed her with a chronic disease that would keep her digestive system extremely vulnerable.

Though she returned home from the hospital, she had to follow a strict diet. The pain in her stomach was a permanent feature! After a couple of months, I returned to Jammu. With the grace of the divine, I had a chance to meet Mohanji again when he visited Jammu. I expressed my concern about Sukriti's situation to him. Mohanji suggested that I ask Sukriti to take 3 Mai-Tri sessions from Subhasree, a Mai Tri practitioner in London. Following Mohanji's advice, Sukriti contacted Subhasree and here is what happened then, as Sukriti herself describes in her words:

"After the diarrhoea incident, I had no energy left. Just walking down a flight of stairs or peeling vegetables would make me overly tired and I would sleep for a couple of hours. While my mother was with me in this period, she was playing the Shiva Kavacham stotram chanted by Mohanji and I would listen to it with her; morning and evening. It gave me a feeling of strength. After my mother left London, life went on and I was trying to control my health condition with diet. I could eat very few things. At one point, I was really fed up. I had been suffering from this condition for the last 12 years. With little children and a job to manage, this condition would leave me totally exhausted at times.

After Mohanji's advice, I went to Subhasree for a Mai-Tri session. In the first session, Subhasree mentioned to me a vision of monkeys and advised me to either offer food to monkeys or chant a Hanuman mantra. That left me speechless because, from my childhood, the only mantra I used to chant was the Hanuman Chaalisa. But for the past few years, I had somehow stopped it. Recently my mother had also advised me to start chanting the Hanuman Chaalisa. I was surprised to hear Subhasree got the same message from the session too. I went home with a feeling of joy. I was feeling much better already!

I went for the second session after a few days and this session was intense. Though my pain had always been in my stomach, during the session, I felt Subhasree's hand strongly on my lower back. She was pressing with her thumb at one point that felt like a huge block of pain. I wondered, how she knew that I had pain exactly at this point, even I didn't realise this earlier. After the session, Subhasree explained to me that she was guided by Mohanji's consciousness to address some blocked energy at that point and this may have caused the pain to appear in my stomach.

When I woke up the next morning, I didn't feel any pain in my stomach! I couldn't believe it! Can it be true that the stomach-ache was gone? It cannot be that easy especially as this pain had been there constantly for years. With disbelief, I even started pinching and pressing my stomach where it used to hurt. Nope. No pain. I even asked my husband to press. Still no pain. I was speechless. This was indeed a miracle that my logical mind was unable to understand. After a few days, I went for the third session, as Mohanji had advised for three sessions of Mai Tri. When I met Subhasree, looking at my smiling face, she was so happy. When I narrated how my pain had vanished, she was speechless and almost had tears. She explained to me that the moment when my mother spoke to him about my *condition and he said about Mai-Tri, from that time itself, his energy had started flowing to me and had been working in my favour. During this period, Mohanji had cleansed a lot of blockages from the past which had appeared as physical pain in this life.*

Subhasree also mentioned that sometimes you get a direction in life and things fall into place with Mohanji's grace. It's more than just the physical aspect of healing. Pain-free and happy, I took this last statement of hers as a motivation. I have always been interested in food as medicine. I soon met someone in London who was an Ayurvedic practitioner and one thing led to another and now I am doing a one year course in Ayurveda. Finally, I realised that with Mohanji's grace, I was not only cured physically, but I also had a new direction in life, learning about this ancient, holistic, healing system – Ayurveda. Thank you Mohanji."

Seeing my daughter Sukriti's recovery and her progress, I feel so blessed to have Mohanji's grace. Not just with Sukriti, Mohanji has given me release from a lingering arthritis pain which had given me a lot of problems. I would love to share this too.

During a recent visit to the UK, I developed severe pain in my left leg. I was not sure if it was because of a Vitamin D deficiency or if my rheumatoid arthritis had made a comeback. My blood tests did not reveal anything problematic.

A few weeks later, I met Mohanji at the Rishikesh Retreat. Whenever I meet him, he would ask me to sit on the chair, rather than on the floor as I would be uncomfortable. I wondered why he never asked about my leg or the limp in it. As I read testimonials of many who have recovered from various illnesses, I would think about myself and also wonder why I did not experience any relief.

In time, my pain became worse, even walking around was difficult. It was becoming impossible to go to school. I tried to ease my pain and improve my mobility using compression socks. My husband supported me immensely by dropping and picking me up from school.

I am also a Mai-Tri practitioner. While performing healing for others, my leg would hurt and it was quite ironical that I was performing healing for others, while in pain! I attributed my pain to my karma and kept going through life.

On the night of January 7th, I saw Mohanji on a chair, like a doctor, examining my leg. I was lying on a bed and appeared to be in great pain. After some time, he asked me to do yoga and added that I would be well. As instructed, I resumed yoga and in just a few days, I became free of pain! Life was normal again.

While Mohanji was visiting Jammu again, one day after a *satsang*, we were discussing issues relating to the school. As we were leaving, Mohanji smilingly reminded me if I wished to say something to him. It was true! I told him that my leg was well after he examined it and that I had no pain now! He said, **"Go tell Chachi Revaji. She keeps complaining that I do not come to Jammu. But I am always there**

for all of you. I may not be here physically, but am here astrally."

Blessed are we to be part of the Mohanji family. My koti koti pranaams to my Guru, who takes care of our physical and our spiritual needs!

Guru Leela

Grace that Heals

THE MAGNIFICENT SURGEON

Preeti Duggal, India

How a Guru protects us and takes care of us is beyond our human minds to understand. He knows what is best for us and delivers at the right time.

My daughter has been dealing with severe auto-immune issues since she was eighteen with very bad skin issues. She has sailed through all these years somehow with Mohanji's grace.

In 2019, her dermatologist in Delhi referred her case to another senior dermatologist in Mumbai for an issue in her body which was not getting cured even after having various rounds of steroids and antibiotics.

When the senior dermatologist saw her condition, she immediately advised us to get a biopsy done for that area. A day before the biopsy, my husband Rajiv messaged Mohanji regarding the procedure to which he replied, **"Don't worry, I'll be there."** As it was a day's procedure, we were allotted a room in the hospital. We entered the room and I pulled off the curtains and to my surprise, I saw an M written on the glass. I knew Mohanji was there with us to which Rajiv then told me about his chat with Mohanji the night before.

The biopsy report came after two weeks and it confirmed carcinoma cells present in her body which just shook us from the inside. Never even in our wildest dreams, we had thought that one day, we would have to deal with such a disease. I immediately called up Madhusudhan Rajagopalan, who is like a younger brother to me as I really needed to talk about it to someone, to understand and accept what I had just read in the report.

He asked me to inform Mohanji about this. Rajiv immediately called Mohanji and told him about the report. Mohanji said, **"You immediately go ahead with the treatment and I will do the best I can for her."** He asked Rajiv to hand over the phone to me. The moment I answered, he said only one sentence to me, **"Duggal, take this entire thing as a project and not as a disease. Don't be emotional or fearful, the more emotional you get, the more it will spread. Just be a support to her and have faith. I will do my best."**

We rushed to Delhi for an appointment with an oncologist in the hospital where she was getting the treatment done for her skin issues. The biggest fear for us was how Riddhima would react when she comes to know about the situation. I kept chanting Mohanji Gayatri and praying to him to give her the strength to deal with it. For a few minutes, she was uncontrollable but then somehow we consoled her to face reality. I was feeling Mohanji's energy with me every moment.

The oncologist referred us to Mumbai for a second opinion as he did not want to rush into any procedure, taking her young age into consideration.

I took the slides and blocks of the biopsy to Mumbai and the histopathology department of two prestigious hospitals famous for their cancer treatments confirmed positive for the carcinoma cells. Then started the rounds of meeting the oncology surgeon, plastic surgeon and various other doctors, pre-surgery tests, and finally, the date was fixed for the 23rd of December for the surgery.

We reached Mumbai on the 21st and on the 22nd afternoon, Riddhima was admitted to the hospital. Riddhima messaged Mohanji for his blessings for the surgery to go smoothly and immediately, he replied: **"Nothing to worry, I'm there with you."**

Early morning of the 23rd, with tears in her eyes, she was wheeled to the OT. My mind was completely blank. No emotions or fears. I was just sitting alone in the hospital room chanting Mohanji's Gayatri. A little later, my husband and other family members joined me in the room. Mohanji had asked Rajiv to inform him about the time of the surgery. Rajiv also mentioned to him that Riddhima wanted to carry Mohanji's eye card with her, but she wasn't allowed, so she was slightly upset. Mohanji responded, **"If I myself am there, why would she need an eye card?"** About an hour later, I just closed my eyes and started chanting the Mai-Tri Gayatri and I could see myself in the operation theatre. Mohanji was standing next to the surgeon and telepathically giving him instructions. I saw him wearing a white kurta, dhoti and a cream shawl. Later in the day, Rajesh confirmed that Mohanji had asked for his white kurta and dhoti while he was packing his clothes, a couple of days earlier, and insisted on taking his white shawl.

The surgery which was planned for six hours was completed in three and a half hours and the doctor came out smiling and fully satisfied. Mohanji as always fulfilled his promise to Riddhima, of being there with her. One just needs to have faith and the Guru delivers much more than what you can even think of. Stop using your mind and doubting, and see how things unfold smoothly. The hiccups come if our faith is not complete or we have a doubt.

Post-surgery, she was discharged after six days and came to stay at Madhusudhan and Preethi G's house as Mohanji had insisted that Riddhima should stay there for her early healing. We finally returned back from Mumbai on 6th January, after getting permission from the doctors.

Today when I look back, I just feel amazed at how this whole episode just ended in a jiffy. No pain, emotions, fears, anger, or agony. Such was the divine force of Mohanji working for us, and the prayers and blessings of all my dear Mohanji family members. My special thanks to Milica who kept doing healings and prayers for her day and night. Madhu, Preethi and their lovely girls stood by us like a rock, with their love and support. That day I realised how blessed and prosperous I am. It is only because of my dear Father Mohanji that everyone kept us in their prayers, taking away some of the pain and we could pass through this ordeal so smoothly.

I have no words to convey my gratitude to him. Every breath is indebted to him. I surrender everything at his lotus feet. I am forever indebted to him for accepting me and holding me always.

FROM DARKNESS TO LIGHT

Rakshitha Ananth, Australia

My Mai-Tri sessions were more than just an experience of deep cleansing or healing. This was the grace and protection of Mohanji that saved my life when I was sinking into darkness. Here is my story of a journey from darkness to light that Mohanji carried me into, through very powerful Mai-Tri sessions.

Somewhere in November 2018, I noticed that I was getting angrier than usual. I attributed it to Consciousness Kriya as I thought that my stored emotions were coming out and that it was a good sign. As much as I tried to watch it and let go, I was seeing that it was consuming me up. By about December 1st week, I was in a rage, with uncontrollable anger towards everyone and everything. I was spitting venom with every word that I spoke to my husband. Because I was aware of my anger, but unable to control it, I decided not to hurt anyone and came out of all social media channels such as WhatsApp, Facebook, etc., and that helped me a bit. Little did I know then that it was all momentary. I continued to be consumed in my anger which went to a point where I was angry with myself. Anger, with guilt added to it, was a perfect recipe that took complete control over me and my emotions, though I was witnessing it. Low self-esteem had always been an issue with me and this added to the other emotions, and it pushed me to a point where I felt I was not worthy in this world and all I wanted to do was to take away my own life including a night dedicated to thinking about the best way to commit suicide.

Every conversation (even an extremely casual one) became a huge fight with my husband. He was very busy with work and Mohanji Foundation as well at that time, and he was unable to devote much time to me, which poured fuel to my anger. I desperately needed some attention from him, which was zero at that point. All my anger was now diverted towards Mohanji as I felt that he was keeping me alive, making me go through so much pain, anger, and suffering. Every time I was angry at him, I was also contemplating on all the good things he brought into my life, all that good stuff that made me what I am today.

However, I felt that Mohanji was the sole reason why my husband wasn't spending any time with me. All these thoughts made me feel angry, unworthy, guilty, and all that I wanted to do at that time was exit this life once and for all so that all this would be over in a matter of hours. I even decided to burn myself as I thought that would leave no trace of me in this world.

While I was going through all of these in stages, I also wanted to immerse myself into some positivity. So I listened to discourses, practised Carnatic music (learning from my mom, who is a professional vocalist herself), started reading 'Autobiography of a Yogi,' increased my chanting, continued with my Kriya, read a few chapters of the Sai Satcharita etc., but I had no desire to talk to anyone about this other than my husband, who turned a deaf ear as he was busy and had no time for me.

While I was trying to keep up with positivity, the anger and negativity were fully consuming me to a point where I lost control of my emotions. Words fail to do justice to explain what I went through, how I felt and most importantly how I was surviving both physically and mentally. I was battling it in my mind and alas, I was waging a lone and a losing battle. I shared my situation with a close Mohanji family member. As much as this person was trying to help me, the guidance and the words spoken made me angrier than ever. So, I decided to shut myself down totally. I lost all strength, fighting this battle alone.

One day, after my Kriya, I prayed to Mohanji to help me come out of this. I said, "I don't want anyone to help me, you come and help me out of this. I don't feel like talking to anyone else." He did hear me I know, because, after a lot of struggle, I felt I should message Milica, a Mai-Tri practitioner, about what was happening.

Milica was very swift in action. We started our Mai-Tri sessions the next day. She saw that I attracted dark energy that was feeding off my anger and made it more profound so that it could survive in me. This energy even tried to cut off our Skype connection and attack Milica, for she was trying to help me out. Finally, Shirdi Sai Baba and Lord Ganesha came and pushed this dark energy away and sent it to the light. This was during the 1st session.

On the 2nd day before the session, I was browsing for

the meaning of Lalitha Sahasranama (1000 names of Shri Lalitha, the most powerful Goddess). I was also internally talking to the Goddess saying, "Why don't you take pity on me and help me out. You see the struggle I am going through. Don't you have any compassion towards me; am I not your child?"

We always have Aum chanting in Mohanji's voice, constantly (on loop) playing near our altar at a medium volume. I had kept the doors of the temple closed so that only a very soft sound of Aum comes out to where I sit. As I was talking to the Goddess, I heard a very loud chant/song – "Ya devi sarva bhutheshu"- a Devi Mantra. I thought it was too loud and possibly coming out of the neighbour's house. But I knew they never play any devotional music. And all the doors and windows of my house were closed, so there was no way that the sound could trickle in this loud into my house.

I listened to it more closely and realised that the song was playing from my meditation hall, that too very loudly. I opened the doors of my temple, ran inside and to my surprise, yes it was playing from our music player. I couldn't believe what was happening. I was trying to analyse it with my logical mind and thought, it must be an error from my player. So, I decided to let it run and came back to my laptop. But suddenly I ran back to the temple, took the player and saw – it was displaying the text – playing AUM Mohanji, but the music being played on the device was, "Ya devi sarva bhuteshu." I paused the music and played it again. This time it played Aum by Mohanji. That is when it struck me that Sri Lalitha Tripura Sundari was showing her presence to me, she had been listening to me. I cried, thanking her and Mohanji for this.

That evening after the session, Milica had tears in her eyes. She said she had never witnessed such deep cleansing. She had a wonderful vision where Mohanji turned into Jesus and held me in his arms. And some divine being that she had never seen, a being so full of love, came and healed my throat chakra. She expressed it in such a way that I couldn't even guess who that divine being could be, one so full of motherly love. But I narrated what happened that afternoon. Tearfully she said – now I know – who else could that divine being be other than the Mother herself. She is the only one who can be so full of love, which words cannot describe.

By about the 2nd session of Mai-Tri, the dark energy completely left me and I felt a lot of relief in general.

It is only through grace that I remembered to surrender to Mohanji and contemplate on the good things he brought into my life. Such awareness would not have happened without his protection and grace. Words can never convey my gratitude towards Mohanji, Para Brahma Swaroopa (the reflection of divine consciousness), without whom I will cease to survive.

Narration from the Mai-Tri Practitioner, Milica

The Mai-Tri session with Rakshitha left me so uplifted and energised that I felt my feet were not touching the ground the whole day long. I was flying in high energies of love.

As we started the session, Mohanji clearly showed me how I was sitting by Rakshitha in her room on the floor, and my body was light with arms outstretched, channelling Mohanji's healing energy to her. Just to explain that I was in Johannesburg and Rakshitha was in Melbourne at that time.

What I was shown was that Rakshitha's throat was cut up and under attack by dark entities. The next scene I witnessed was of Mohanji coming towards us, enveloped in a bright white and golden light. Suddenly his face turned into the face of Jesus and he took Rakshitha into his arms and healed her. Mohanji, the shield of protection, everywhere, all the time!

The light was blinding and the energy was so powerful. I felt that in the presence of such light, no negativity can survive. That's exactly what happened after the Mai-Tri! The darkness was gone! Moving to the heart centre, I felt an explosion of love so intense that it enveloped me too, and filled us both up. It is love that heals, aligns and completes.

Only after talking to Rakshitha, I realised it was Divine Mother's presence as she had sincerely prayed to her before the healing. All that happened was deeply transformative and healing. This was possible only due to the grace and power of Mohanji. Thank you Mohanji for your love and protection!

Guru Leela

Grace that Heals

ANCHORED IN LOVE

Rekha Murali, India

Mohanji's compassion has no boundaries. This is what I experienced in my initial interactions with Mohanji. When he says, **"I am with you,"** he really means it. These are not mere words; the extent to which he clears us empties us of all the samskaras (impressions, karmic baggage) to fill us with the divine, can be realised only to a very small extent. For a gross mind such as mine to recognise this, it took two years!

Since 2013, I had been suffering from severe low back pain caused by a nerve prolapse requiring surgery. The doctor had warned me that I needed to be very careful and had put me on medications to prolong the inevitable. But there was a pattern to the pain. Every six months from thereon, it would start hurting and I would be bed-ridden for nearly a month, unable to take care of my basic needs. I was on alternate healing and allopathy during this time.

In 2015, I met Mohanji and soon after started communicating with him through chats. The following year (2016), I was bracing myself for another painful relapse of the back pain and it happened. I would just lie on my bed crying and mentally pleading with Mohanji to remove the pain. Once while on a real chat with him, I mentioned my condition to him for the first time, and added that I was going wrong somewhere. He said,

> "You are going wrong nowhere. You need to tame your mind which is overworked. Connect to me more intensely. Leave your mind with me. And when you detach your mind from your pain, the pain will reduce."

Although I knew that he was right, at that point, the pain was unbearable, and my mind seemed to take control. How do I detach from the mind, particularly when bedridden and unable to even turn or move? It is then that the mind becomes overactive and plants its seeds. Little did I know then, that he had been working on me as promised and had removed a lot of blockages from the mind and body!

Soon after, Mohanji came to Chennai (where I live) and he sent word that he would like to meet me. I still had back pain but could move around gently. Luckily for me, he was staying at my sister's place and my sister asked me to spend the night there too. Surprisingly, I had no pain when I was in his energy field. I took his blessings and to my astonishment, I was able to offer my pranaams (prostrations) at his feet, which until that moment was an impossible task. I assisted my sister with serving him and spent a blissful evening. Again I was totally unaware, that he was working on me and healing my condition. The next morning, in a gentle and loving voice, Mohanji asked me how my back was. I was feeling so happy that I could not even reply and showed him the thumbs-up sign! My heart was filled with gratitude and bliss. He then left for his next destination.

Thereafter, I recovered completely within a month and was able to resume most of my other activities, including driving. But the most beautiful part is that since then for the last two years, I have not had a single attack of back pain! In such a casual way, Mohanji held my hand, carried me through a difficult part of my life, and showered me with his healing, blessings and love. I am forever grateful to him. He taught me the biggest lesson in life – to let go of the mind!

Since then, whenever the mind takes charge, I try to push it back as his words resonate within me.

> "Pain is in the body. Suffering is in the mind. Why should pain affect the mind when your mind is connected to me? You can convert every pain to karmic relief by detaching your mind from it. I am with you."

Mohanji is our Anchor, carrying us through the turbulence of life, doing his job thoroughly for our highest good. His compassion and unconditional love can only be experienced as it can never be described in words. He ceaselessly works to help every soul that is connected to him. Tears of gratitude flow as I connect with him and surrender to his will!

Soon in 2018, Mohanji empowered me as his Acharya. As a Mohanji Acharya, I seem to come across various incidents and people who desperately cry out for his help. This brought into focus other incidents in the past four years where I have been an instrument to reach out to people who needed him.

Let me share a major incident which was an eye-opener for me and the people involved in it. Mohanji's magic wand is what brought a friend out of the deep and dark wood that she found herself in. I am not revealing the name of the person concerned as what matters is not the name but the work of the Guru. It highlights the importance of a living Master in our lives and the only thing we can do is hold on to this anchor.

This friend changed from a chirpy, friendly person to a completely depressed soul overnight. She surrendered completely to the dark forces in her mind, neglecting her family and friends. Life turned topsy-turvy for the entire family and all hell broke loose. I started counselling her, thinking that it would help and not understanding the severity of her condition. Medical help was sought and she was put on medication. There was no one to even monitor if she was taking her medications regularly. Without getting into details of the agony and pain suffered by her and her family, it was then I reached out to Mohanji, feeling helpless and worried. He barely knew her (in this lifetime at least) but set to work on her. Connecting to the eye card would have helped but she was in no condition to do it. He advised me to take her to temples, increase her bhakti while he relentlessly worked on her for two whole years. He invited her for a retreat which helped him heal her rapidly. The first time (as there were repeats of the attack), she came out of her condition within 4 months and that is when she attended the retreat.

A year later, the depression set in again but by then she had received Shaktipat and healing from Mohanji. This time, it was only a clearing of the few traces embedded in her. She was by then deeply connected to Mohanji and since 2017, she has been completely cured and is now leading a happy and fulfilling life with her family.

Having witnessed this success story, I can strongly say with conviction that it was a miracle - It was Mohanji's healing and protection that brought her back on her feet and once again helped her hold the reins of the household.

Soon after, I became a Mai-Tri practitioner and have seen the miraculous ways through which Mohanji operates. It is indeed magical! A recent incident was that of a 71-year-old lady who recovered speedily through the distance Mai-Tri Method. I got a call from a friend of our Mohanji family asking for distance healing for her aunt who was in the ICU having blood clots in her brain causing repeated falls.

It was amazing how Mohanji worked on her aunt during the first session. Mohanji ensured that I focussed on the region of the head and he revealed two big clots there. I also saw a bluish yellow light entering the two clots. When I checked with my friend, she did confirm that there were two clots in her aunt's brain which were not disintegrating.

During the second session, Mohanji showed me just one very small clot. Unfortunately after that, the patient developed a severe headache and we had the third session the next day. This was so miraculous as I saw her brain cut open as though some surgery was being done.

Surprisingly this surgery was not done by the doctors but by our healer Mohanji! She was discharged from the hospital that afternoon without surgery. What I had seen was Mohanji working on her, healing her with his powerful and divine energy. Little do we know the way he operates – it is subtle and beautiful with no discomfort to the patient. I was left speechless!

Physical healing such as mine, a deep mental depression as that of my friend's or an intense surgery as that of this aunt, our beloved Mohanji takes care, selflessly and with no expectations. Be it physical, emotional, mental or spiritual baggage that we carry over lifetimes, it is Mohanji's grace that heals and protects us. All that we have to do is stay connected with him with faith and the conviction that he will carry us towards our chosen path. It is indeed grace that heals. My heart overflows with gratitude as I realise the magnitude of the grace that he showers on us!

A PRECIOUS GIFT

Saakshi Gupta, India

My daughter Gauranghi is a gift from Mohanji. We were trying for a baby for two years, without any results. Then one day, Mohanji told me, **"I can see that a baby is coming, you should prepare yourself for the baby."** Like he said, within two months, I became pregnant. Then the real trial started. From the second month onwards, major complications happened due to ruptured membranes. It is extremely rare for a baby to survive something like this so early in a pregnancy. Even my gynaecologist was amazed at how the baby was surviving in spite of so many complications. On hearing their concern, I would reassure myself that Mohanji was taking care.

Although Mohanji was physically not in India, whenever I was worried that the pregnancy would not continue, he would message me or assure me in some way that everything will be alright. These timely reassurances gave me immense strength during this extremely worrying period.

In my eighth month, I had a dream where I saw many people saying that this baby was not going to survive. But I also saw that Mohanji was holding a small baby in his arms and smiling. Looking straight into my eyes, he said, **"Don't worry your baby is safe and will be with you safe and sound."** This is the power and magic of my Master!

Finally, my delivery date was getting closer. One

day I received a message from Mohanji asking me, **"Where are you?"** I said I'm at home, and he replied, **"Go and admit yourself in the hospital. The baby will be out soon!"** It was 2 p.m. I was shocked at this sudden and unexpected message and called my husband. He said, "Don't worry I will be home soon."

Within half an hour, I was admitted to the hospital. Mohanji told me clearly, "I'm with you." My doctor was surprised at our sudden arrival and asked us what's happening. Within a few minutes, my pains started and in two hours my baby was delivered! It was a normal delivery without any complications. I had a healthy baby with a normal weight.

In my delivery room, I saw Mohanji and Baba Sai. They were both there, taking care of me. It all happened super-fast! My God, even today, when I recall those moments, I get goosebumps. This is how Mohanji works. So unconditional, so loving, and works silently as always to protect us.

I would like to share another experience of his loving protection. How Mohanji works and how he goes out of his way to help his devotees is beyond explanations.

There was some renovation work going on at my house. It was evening, so the carpenter and his team had already finished their work for the day. Two new windows were made for my daughter's room. My daughter Swasti was playing in the garden along with her younger sister. She was very excited to see what the carpenter had done that day. So she went near the new window to open it in great excitement. But as luck would have it, the window was not nailed in and fell straight on my daughter's right toe.

I was sitting in the other corner of the garden. She came running towards me crying, "Mama, my foot, I can't even move it." I pacified her and gave her some water, but she was crying so loudly in pain that even I couldn't hold back my tears.

My husband and I took her to our bedroom and there I saw Mohanji's picture. I started chanting and requested Mohanji to give her strength. I immediately messaged Mohanji about Swasti. Within one minute, he texted back, **"Don't worry, I will do something. Give her vibhuti."**

The moment I messaged Mohanji, Swasti stopped crying. I could feel his presence. I texted Mohanji that Swasti was settling down. He told me, **"I can see. I have placed my hands on her feet."** Within five minutes, Swasti started smiling and she was comfortable.

It was magical and it was the healing touch of my Mohanji that did wonders. My daughter who was crying loudly had settled down within 10 minutes, smiling. As per our routine, we did our evening aarati to Mohanji, with tears of gratitude.

Next day, our doctor suggested an X-ray as there was swelling. So we went for an X-ray. Everyone was sure that there would be a fracture in her toe. But when your Master heals, nothing can touch you, not even the weight of a 50 kg heavy window.

With great difficulty but with the strength of my Mohanji, I took Swasti to the X-ray clinic. At first glance, the doctor said that there was a fracture. She placed Swasti's foot on the table. I started chanting Mohanji's Gayatri and closed my eyes.

When I opened my eyes, I could see that the doctor was shocked. She was taking multiple pictures and close-ups. I asked her if everything was alright. She said, "How's it possible? It's impossible. With so much swelling, there is no fracture?" She took a couple of more close-ups. Nothing was there. She then called her senior doctor. He saw her foot. He was sure of a fracture. Then he took pictures and I knew whose touch had created the magic. It was my father, Mohanji, for sure.

After taking so many pictures, the senior doctor wanted to take a picture of the other foot to compare. I was smiling as I knew now that these guys were confused. Mohanji's magic and his healing touch was the power behind Swasti's recovery.

The senior doctor took many pictures but there appeared to be no cracks in the bone. Then he finally decided and declared that a crack may not be there. I could see the shock on both the doctors' faces!

Now, Swasti is much better. Since no crack was visible, the doctor told me it was a hair-line fracture and Swasti is recovering beautifully with the grace and blessings of my Guruji Mohanji. The only reason behind her recovery and healing was my Guru's healing touch. Nothing can harm us when we have grace and blessings from our Guru. Love and gratitude always!

INVISIBLE EMBRACE
Subhasree Thottungal, UK

Recovering from Rheumatoid Arthritis by Mohanji's grace, in his physical presence, through attending his retreats and walking on the selfless path of service shown by him were my experiences of personal transformation. I have written about it in Guru Leela Volume 2. But as you know, when we get connected to a Guru, not just us but our family, our lineage, our forefathers, even our future generations also receive the protection of the Guru. I have experienced this grace of protection amongst my family members too. Mohanji has always held not just me but my entire family in his invisible embrace, very lovingly and compassionately. I share here two such stories that have brought complete clarity to me about the eternal protection and grace that comes through this connection with conviction and surrender to Guru.

Healing for my father-in-law

2nd January 2016. We were at my in-laws' place in Kerala for Christmas vacation. There was a sudden opportunity to meet Mohanji at his home in Palakkad, Kerala. Having missed the opportunity to visit Jagannath Temple in Puri, a few days back in Odisha, I felt that Lord Jagannath had allowed me to feel his presence through meeting Mohanji. I was still in disbelief that I was actually going to meet Mohanji, at his home! What a blessing that his parental home is just about 15 minutes away from my in-laws' place! This would be my second meeting with Mohanji, having met him for the first time in London just about 5 months back, in July 2015.

Well, nothing is ever a coincidence! It was indeed a divine plan for a much bigger purpose!

This vacation wasn't very easy. We had recently found that my father-in-law's cancer had relapsed after 4 years of treatment, in a pretty bad way. There was literally no hope; no medicine could work as the cancer had found its way around it! Well, there was a small hope with a huge risk. A medicine, which had been started just 2 years back in the USA, still in development in the UK and Europe, was the only option. But it was almost a next to impossible option. This medicine was available only in the USA and needed to be imported from there every 4 to 6 weeks (that would last 2 cycles of treatment), and hence had a roaring high cost! If this worked, it would be the only possible chance to keep my father-in-law alive. That meant we were talking about a long term treatment and hence the financial affordability for such an arrangement seemed like a mountainous task. Not only this, the new age of the medicine also brought a threat to life, almost instant, within 48 hours, in case it didn't agree with the patient's body. While our hearts were saying to give it a go, solving the financial issues later, the mind was scaring us with this humongous threat. Such a situation brought not just dilemma but immense stress to us as a family. We could of course not disclose the full story to my mother-in-law! Having the whole family on vacation with her sons and grandchildren, my mother-in-law was enjoying every moment without having the slightest idea of what dilemma her sons were going through.

Amidst this situation at home, I got the golden opportunity to meet Mohanji. When the time came, I went to meet Mohanji along with my mother-in-law. This was the first time my mother-in-law was meeting Mohanji and she had no clue of the stature of Mohanji. For her, he was just another famous person, whom we met in London. While I was still trying to pinch myself to believe that I was really sitting in front of Mohanji and feeling the divinity of Lord Jagannath, my mother-in-law was happily conversing with Mohanji's mother. Then, I only had one silent thought and a sincere prayer to Mohanji, "Please let this smile on Amma stay like this. Let the dark clouds of risk for Achhan's life not hide her smile. Let the new medicine work for Achhan positively." Then, I had no clue that Mohanji hears all my thoughts! We returned from Mohanji's house. I returned to London.

We decided to go ahead with the new medication. Miraculously, some blocked investments were released and we managed to arrange the money required for the treatment. Cycle after cycle, the medicine continued. Of course, it suited my father-in-law. His condition started to improve. The threat to his life had disappeared. Money for the treatment was getting arranged. What had seemed like next to impossible was actually happening! Day by day, Achhan was getting back to normal life. As each day passed, I started to realise that this was no less than a miracle. This was the answer from Mohanji for my prayers, "Let the smile on my mother-in-law's face continue." He had made everything feel so smooth, so easy, but silently! No one in my family, not even my husband knew about my silent prayer and had no clue that something impossible like this was happening. Probably even taken for granted, the grace had gone unnoticed. But the picture was quite clear to me.

Jan 2018. Exactly 2 years later. After having a nearly normal life in those two years, suddenly Achhan caught a nasty infection and developed renal failure. Just about 2 hours before I was about to take off on the flight to Mumbai to attend the Yoga Teachers training course in Ganeshpuri, we received a call informing us that Achhan was in the ICU! It was too late for me to change the plan. So we decided that I will go ahead and when I reach Mumbai, depending on his status, either I will go to the hospital or continue with my yoga training.

Before going to Ganeshpuri for the yoga training, I had a plan to go to Shirdi since Mohanji would be there for a day. I would have a chance to meet him, and of course the chance to visit Shirdi Sai Baba's Samadhi temple after 13 years. Now with the sudden twist in my father-in-law's condition, I was doubtful that I could go to Shirdi. However, I surrendered at the feet of my Guru and Baba Sai. When I landed in Mumbai and called my in-laws, I found out that he was still in ICU, but there was nothing I could do by going to the hospital (this was in a different city from my in-laws' place and hence it wasn't easy to just go and stay there). My brother-in-law was there. So I proceeded to Shirdi and felt that being in the presence of Baba and Mohanji, my prayers for Achhan would be more fruitful.

After the temple visit, I met Mohanji and conveyed to him my father-in-law's serious condition and the agony that my husband and the whole family were going through. After I narrated everything, I saw Mohanji go quiet and then he said slowly, **"His soul is not interested in staying anymore. The soul is looking forward to the exit."** I was dumbstruck. Silent exclamations, "Oh no! Harish will be devastated to hear this. Mohanji, please do something!" Mohanji hears every unuttered word too. He said, **"Let us see what we can do."** This statement was enough! I knew everything would be taken care of.

While I went ahead for the yoga training that day in Ganeshpuri, I was in constant touch with my brother-in-law about Achhan's state. He said the doctor had advised him to be in the ICU for a minimum of 3 weeks and that they would start the treatment there. 3 weeks in the ICU! Fear was trickling in! My husband in London was also getting worried. In this situation, my faith was only on Mohanji. The words, "We will see what we can do" were ringing in my ears. Also Mohanji's assurance that whenever doubt or fear crops up, we need to look back at all the previous experiences and remember how he has always been with us. 3 days after coming to Ganeshpuri, an update came from the hospital. Achhan was shifted from the ICU to a normal ward! What? The doctor had said minimum 3 weeks in ICU! And on the 3rd day, he was out of the ICU. It wasn't difficult for me or Harish to realise that this wasn't a simple ordinary phenomenon. Mohanji's grace was at work! Finally, after my completion of yoga training, I went back to London and Harish travelled to India to be with his father in the hospital. Achhan was in a normal ward and dialysis was still going on. Doctors were committing to nothing! Suddenly, after a few days, I got a message that Achhan was discharged from the hospital and was returning home. And that was exactly during the 3rd week!

So, during the 3 weeks that he was originally going to be in the ICU, he actually fully recovered and was back home! Harish and I realised that this miraculous healing from the near death condition due to kidney failure was surely Mohanji's grace. Just remember, he was still under that special cancer treatment!

After this incident, it was as if he got a new life! He was full of energy, and was performing all activities as if he didn't even have cancer. Many unfinished issues were completed. He lived a healthy normal life for the next 10 months. His soul which was ready to leave the body a long time ago, probably stayed back to finish some of the pending jobs it had, and with divine grace, had a smooth exit later, without much pain.

Not only did Mohanji ensure that after the incident, he had a healthy life, when he left, it was a smooth exit.

When I look back at my father-in-law's journey from Jan 2016 (since I met Mohanji at his home) till Achhan left his body in Dec 2018, his life was blessed with divine grace. And for Harish and me, this divine grace was all due to none other than our Mohanji.

Healing for my brother

Words are not required to express our thoughts and feelings when we have the connection in consciousness! With Mohanji, most of the time, we don't even need to ask anything physically. He hears our thoughts and does what he needs to do. When he says, **"I do my job"**, he does that.

This personal experience that I am going to share with you is something that amuses me every time I remember this, and gives us a glimpse of the vast ocean of grace and compassion called Mohanji.

Back in 2017, one day I heard from my brother who is just about 4 years older than me, in his 40s, that he has been diagnosed with a rare genetic heart problem which could suddenly cause a cardiac arrest. The moment I heard this, my immediate call from the heart was to Mohanji. Within minutes, I felt Mohanji's assurance in the consciousness. I felt and heard his words, "We will do whatever we can."

Meanwhile, a few doctors whom my brother consulted, and even a doctor friend of ours in London, advised him to visit one of the best heart specialists in India, especially for this particular condition and to get a surgery done. He was told that it was best to get the surgery done at the earliest, as the risk could happen any time. This was indeed a stressful time for all of us. I kept praying to Mohanji in silence.

Sometime later, I had the opportunity to be with Mohanji in Novi Sad and on the same morning I arrived there, my brother messaged me that he was visiting a top specialist that day and he was ready with everything if the operation needed to happen immediately. After getting this message, my heart started beating faster. When I got a chance to speak to Mohanji, I told him about my brother's situation and showed him my brother's photo in my mobile. Mohanji blessed his photo and said "We will see what we can do." This sentence was reassuring, as I know when Mohanji says this, all problems go away. I was confident that Mohanji would be with my brother during the operation, his operation would be successful, and he'd recover soon.

The day passed, busy with the events with Mohanji and I had no chance of seeing my phone that day. Later in the night when I retired to my room, I opened my phone and saw a message from my brother. Reading that message, I literally jumped out of my bed. I couldn't believe what my eyes were reading! My brother had written that earlier in the day when he met the specialist, the specialist had checked everything and concluded that my brother didn't need an operation; they could treat him with medicines and re-check after 3 months!

I was praying for a successful operation, as that was inevitable from all the previous doctors' advice and I was sure that when Mohanji blessed his photo, he would ensure the surgery to be successful. It was beyond my imagination that Mohanji would totally dissolve the question of surgery.... No surgery required!!! It was nearly midnight and even after the whole day's busy schedule, I had no tiredness. My sleepiness had gone; I couldn't wait to meet

Mohanji in the morning! I expressed my gratitude for this miracle in the consciousness and also through a text message! Finally, when I met Mohanji in the morning with his morning tea, I bowed down at his feet. How else can I express my deepest gratitude to my Gurudev who had done this miracle! "What can I do Mohanji?" I asked him with tears of overflowing emotions. Very calmly he said, **"Ask your brother to feed fishes, birds and animals. Nature and the beings will protect him. Nature is protecting him."**

I melted even more. He knows what a relief it was to hear the miraculous news of no surgery required, and there was nothing in return he asked for himself! He simply asked to feed the beings in the nature! My heart was expanding even more at seeing the true and unconditional love in Mohanji. What can we even give him? He asks nothing. He needs nothing. He can have everything, but he truly needs nothing.

It's more than 2 years now and the feeling of that day is still fresh in my memory. With his grace, my brother is keeping well. I know now, when we are connected to Mohanji, our family, and our entire lineage has the highest protection of the Tradition.

With a heart full of love, eyes brimming with tears of joy, my head bows down again at the feet of my Guru, my father, my mother, my best friend, and my beloved, whom I call "Mohanji."

Guru Leela

Grace that Heals

A WALK OF FAITH

Sunita Madan, India

The Bosnian Pyramid Pilgrimage and the Kriya Intensive Programme were the first of my long retreats with Mohanji. The Bosnian Pyramids have always been a mystery to me, I have always wanted to be there and experience them first hand rather than reading others' experiences. But more than the pyramids, the thought of being with Mohanji for nearly 10 days was like a dream. There were many issues and obstacles before I boarded the aircraft towards Istanbul and finally Sarajevo. I was finally there. I shared a room on the 5th floor of the hotel and I got to know that Mohanji was on the 6th floor. The thought itself kindled all kinds of emotions! The following day was to be the satsang and there I saw my Father, my Mohanji, full of unconditional love as he shared a word or a hug with one and all. When it was my turn, I waited for the hug which was a dream come true. It made me feel so loved and complete.

The next day was our pilgrimage to the Sun Pyramid. Now came all the challenges. It was to be a long walk uphill and then a steep climb. I wondered if I had been wise to agree to climb up. Fortunately, I reached a certain point by car, but then the next stage was the steep climb. Mohanji had led the way and one by one, slowly but surely, everyone was climbing up. I started the climb one step at a time, chanting the Mohanji Gayatri in my mind.

Dear George guided me beautifully, encouraging me at every step. I slowly and steadily moved up, having to stop after every three steps to take a deep breath. My main thought at the time was, "Will I ever make it?" As this thought came to me, I looked up and saw my Guru, my Master, looking down at me. My fear reduced and I immediately knew that he was taking care of me. It was his grace that I was in Bosnia and it was his grace that I could move and go up the steep path of the Bosnian Pyramids. Due to a slipped disc issue, I normally have to be very careful with my knees, my legs and my back. And here I was, climbing a pyramid many metres high. This was indeed a miracle.

When I reached Mohanji later, I thanked him and he said, "You are doing well." Anything and everything can happen with the Master's grace and in my case; his grace flowed all the way. I was encouraged to climb further up where we gathered to meditate. His grace continued to flow as we went up the Moon Pyramid as well. The vehicle in which we travelled to the Moon Pyramid had a high step. It was very difficult for me to climb up and also to get down. Mohanji held my hand as I was wondering how to get down and then he said, "Jump!" It was a direct command from my Guru. Without a thought about my knees, my legs and my back, I simply jumped and lo and behold, I landed on my feet safely, and all my aches and pains vanished!

Today when I look back, I am in awe that I managed to do all of this and know that it was only possible with Mohanji's grace and blessings. I feel deep gratitude and deep love for my Guru who held my hand and blessed me with the words, **"I am always there with you."**

With such physical pain and inability, travelling all the way to Bosnia, followed by the climb to the Pyramids, connecting to the energies and meditating there had not been my cup of tea. But, lifetimes of karmas have been washed away in this pilgrimage and this was made possible only because of Mohanji.

Without much ado to whatever he does, he works silently, effortlessly and very smoothly. The transformation in our lives and the deep cleansing we receive are phenomenal. To my Guru of such stature, the only thing I can give is my humble prostrations at his holy feet. Jai Jai Jai Gurudeva.

THE UNSEEN HEALER
Tina Arya, USA

Mai-Tri Method is a very powerful healing modality and as Mohanji says, it's a healing method of the White Path. Mohanji's divine energy is blessing people with miracles and as a witness, I am blown away by these miracles.

I was approached by an acquaintance at the end of December to do Mai-Tri for her husband. He had stage 4 pancreatic cancer and was bedridden. When I went to their home for the first session, he was mentally alert but had multiple complications because of the disease. He had severe oedema in his legs and could not walk without support. Mohanji guided me and told me that he will get better only if oedema goes down. So I told his wife that she should consult with the doctors to make sure that the excess build-up of fluid was drained with the help of medications. At this time, doctors were saying that his condition was not treatable and they can only keep him comfortable.

We had 4 sessions of Mai-Tri Method and during the last session at his home, he drifted in and out of sleep and his condition seemed to be getting worse. His wife was not able to take care of him and Mohanji again guided me during the process to have him shifted to a hospice. After 3 days, I went to do Mai-Tri at the hospice and his condition was much worse, he was barely conscious and his wife said he had stopped eating 2 days back. He had also stopped talking.

His parents called up to video chat with him as I entered the room, so I went out to give him privacy. When the call was over, his wife came out and said that she wasn't even sure if he could hear his parents, let alone recognise them. Then I went in to give him Mai-Tri and as I was moving along the third eye and throat chakra, he said, "I want water." His wife was shocked as he had not spoken for two days. He was so weak at this time that he was being fed through a syringe, and swallowing even 5 ml of water took him about 20 seconds. So I stopped, and his wife gave him some water. As I passed energy along the throat and heart chakras, he made a loud sound as if he was in pain, so I stopped again and asked him if he was in pain and he said, "No, I am not in pain, I feel uncomfortable as if something is holding me down." Hearing this, his wife was speechless.

There was more guidance from Mohanji during Mai-Tri about reducing his pain medication. I completed the session and he calmed down and slept. His wife and I stepped out to talk. She told me that the hospice director said that looking at all the symptoms and his condition; he was not going to live for more than 1 or 2 days. I gave her Mohanji's messages but she didn't sound very hopeful at that time.

Amazingly, he started getting better from that day. He started eating with a spoon within a couple of days. His appetite grew and he became mentally alert. It has been two months since I did Mai-Tri for him at the hospice. Doctors and health care professionals had said that he was not going to make it. He is getting better every day and his wife is going to move him to a rehab centre so he can be on his feet again. His oedema is completely gone but his muscles are weak, so he needs physical therapy. There were so many times that this person seemed to be getting worse but survived way beyond all the doctors' expectations.

As a Mai-Tri Method practitioner, I was a witness to these amazing miracles. We are so blessed to be connected to Mohanji and to be given this platform to serve. I have felt my faith and surrender grow exponentially since I was initiated into Mai-Tri Method. My connection to Mohanji has become deeper. My eternal gratitude to Mohanji for his guidance.

COSMIC WINK

Charice Bhardwaj, UK

As I sit down to write this, I feel the pressure of trying to describe something which is so much more vast than me, to attempt the important task of articulating the Master's 'Grace' — something which should be done with care and seriousness.

Then, as my fingertips approach the keyboard, I glance through the window and across the street, I see a middle-aged man standing on the roof of his shed with his fists on his hips, wearing strange little shorts in this freezing January climate. He looks perfectly ridiculous - like a schoolboy pretending to fly! I laugh, forgetting all about the seriousness of this writing task, and the words begin to effortlessly flow...

This is how Mohanji's grace falls on me. He always appeals to my playful, creative constitution, the part of me which sees these snapshots of life as material for a show, as the juice of creativity. Mohanji has a way of making me laugh at myself when I am taking life too seriously. I might call this the 'cosmic joke' factor.

Just half an hour ago, I was very distressed about that man across the street because he kept looking at me through my window. Many fears flashed through my mind about old men preying on young women like me, and I was feeling deeply uncomfortable at being watched in my own home. Moments later, this clownish image is revealed to me; a grown man in little shorts bizarrely standing on his own roof in the middle of winter, looking like the least threatening person ever. In an instant, all my fears are cancelled out and lightness rushes in. I asked for Mohanji's protection, and he responded with a cosmic wink. I see this as part of the Master's grace because it is protection through laughter – the lightness through which we regain our power, sanctity and joy.

Grace flows through humour because it pulls the rug of concepts from underneath our feet and forces us to challenge our own expectations. Once, at the sacred gardens by the Bosnian Pyramids, the pilgrims were cleansing in the spiralling rock formations and meditating in their high vibrations. Some stopped by a large boulder to place their hands on it and absorb its energies. Mohanji joined the circle and placed his palm on it. We all closed our eyes with deep intention and seized the opportunity to participate in whatever he was doing. Sounds of "Mmmm" and "Wow, so amazing" arose from the circle. We opened our eyes and saw Mohanji nod. Someone asked, "What do you feel, Mohanji?"

"Absolutely nothing", he replied, "this one is just for decoration."

Our performances of sincere pilgrim hood were hilariously undercut by Mohanji's bluntness and cheekiness in humouring our display of 'spirituality.' The vulnerability, truth and authenticity of that embarrassing moment allowed us to simply be. How many lessons are delivered through these 'cosmic jokes!' Do we dare bear witness to the humour of the universe? Do we have the humility to delight in the Master's wit? This is grace that heals.

Grace that Heals

Guru Leela

WOH SAANS

Devotional Song – Jyoti Bahl

Hindi	English
Who saans kis kaam ki , jismein tumhara naam na ho Mohan Who baat kis kaam ki, jismein tumhara zikra na ho Mohan	What is the use of that breath, if your name is not in it, Mohan What is the purpose of that chat, if you are not mentioned in it, Mohan
Jai Jai Mohan	Hail to Mohan
Sabko sahara diya hai, tumne kinara diya hai (2) Jab meri baari aayi, tumne kyuon nazrein churayi (2) Tumhri sharan mein mein aayi, Mujhe apanalo hai Mohan	You have given protection to all, you have guided us to the shore When it was my turn, why did you turn away? I seek solace at your feet Accept me Mohan
Jai Jai Mohan	Hail to Mohan
Tum mere Mohan SHyaam Ho Tum Mere parna adhaar	You are my loving Lord Krishna You are the foundation of my life
Duniya se kuchh na chahun Chahun tumhara dular Duniya se kuchh na chahun Maangu tumhara dular Naiya tumre hawale Paar laga do hey Mohan	I have no expectations from the world All I seek is your love I have no expectations from the world All I ask is your love The boat is in your control Make it reach the shore, O Mohan
Jai Jai Mohan	Hail to Mohan

Guru Leela

Ghanaghor andhera chhaya	When there was darkness everywhere
Mann mera ghabaraya	When fear engulfed my mind
Tab tumne raah dikhayi	You showed me the path
Saburi ki jyot jalayi	You lit the lamp of patience within me
Reham woh karam barasao	Always shower your blessings
Hum sab par mere Mohan	On all of us, O Mohan
Jai Jai Mohan	Hail to Mohan

You can watch the video of this devotional song through this link

https://youtu.be/2YfItNT2MhE

Sung by Jyoti Bahl
Video by Neelima Vepu

Grace that Heals

MOHANJI GAYATRI MANTRA

*Om Tatpurushaaya Vidmahe
Hridaya Vasaaya Dheemahi
Mohan: Shankara Prachodayaat*

I recognize the pure formless,
As the One who resides in my heart,
May Mohanji, my Shiva enlighten me.